BASKET
of
BLESSINGS

BASKET
of
BLESSINGS

40 DAYS

to a more *grateful* heart

KAREN O'CONNOR

LIVING
INK
BOOKS
Writing Worth Reading

An Imprint of AMG Publishers

Cover designed by Meyers Design, Houston, Texas
Interior design and typesetting by Reider Publishing Services,
    West Hollywood, California
Edited and Proofread by Jennifer Ball, Dan Penwell, Donna Clark Goodrich,
    and Rick Steele

Printed in the United States of America

ISBN: 0-7394-6428-0

To my parents, Eva and Phil O'Connor,
who showed me what it means to live with a heart of gratitude.

Acknowledgments

I am grateful to my husband, Charles,
the staff of AMG, especially Dan Penwell,
and to friends and family who encouraged me to write this book.

Contents

x

PART THREE
CONTINUING THE JOURNEY

TREASURES OF
THE HEART

Introduction
Cultivating a Grateful Heart

 A GRATEFUL HEART is a gift from God. Left to our own initiative, we might never develop one. We can always find something to complain about or to improve. Criticism has its place. Change is often a good thing. But life is full of blessings as well, from a warm pool of morning sun on a bedroom carpet to the shimmering lights reflected on a rain-soaked neighborhood street; from a child snuggled in our lap to a brand-new car in the driveway.

We can be grateful for the unexpected: a note from an old friend with whom we've lost touch or a word of encouragement from a person we hardly know. We can be grateful for beauty: the fresh face of a baby after a long nap or water droplets resting on a red rose after a rain. We can be grateful for pain: the death of a loved one, a divorce, or an illness—each a gift in its own way, if we take time to see it.

We can be grateful for the predictable: hot cereal with cinnamon every morning or a sunny day in southern California. We can be grateful for the unpredictable: our spouse's mood, the weather, our own feelings. People. Places. Experiences. All give us reasons to be grateful. How different our lives would be if we turned our hearts toward gratitude—not just occasionally, as on Thanksgiving Day or Mother's Day. And not just a greeting-card kind of thanks, but a genuine gratefulness that expresses itself in a hymn of heartfelt praise to God.

What would happen if we cultivated a daily habit of expressing gratitude, one that helped us count all of life good, regardless of the circumstances? When we experience gratitude in a profound way, it not only changes us, it also spills over onto other people.

My father-in-law, Charlie Flowers, often told a story that illustrates this point well. On Christmas morning in 1912 in Paducah, Kentucky, Charlie and his three brothers and two sisters huddled in their beds, fully dressed, trying to keep warm as the wind howled outside their small frame house. It was a desperate time for their family. The coal had run out. There was little money—none for gifts.

Their tree, made from scraps of colored paper and received the night before, was a gift from a local merchant who "couldn't sell this last one." Earlier that year their father had died. To pass the time, the children joked and shouted stories to one another across the hallway. Suddenly they heard a racket from the alley in the back of their house.

"Charlie," his mother called, "would you see what's going on out there?"

Charlie pulled on his shoes and ran out back. There stood a man in a wagon bent over a load of coal, shoveling it into the shed as fast as he could. "Hey Mister, we didn't order any coal!" Charlie shouted. "You're delivering it to the wrong house."

"Your name's Flowers, isn't it?" the man asked, still shoveling. Charlie nodded. "Well then, there's no mistake. I've been asked to deliver this to your family on Christmas morning." Then he turned and looked the awe-struck boy square in the eye. "And I'm under strict orders not to tell who sent it," he teased.

"Gosh, Mister, thanks. Thanks a lot!" Charlie shouted before running into the house to share the news with his family.

Charlie Flowers lived to be ninety-six, and every Christmas he told the story of that sub-zero Christmas morning when two strangers gave his family an unforgettable gift. With coal to warm them (perhaps even to save their lives), a small tree to gather around and each other to hold on to, Charlie and his siblings no longer focused on what they lacked: a dad to play and snuggle with, presents to open and money to spend. That day God not only filled their coal bin, He also filled their hearts. He became their provider in an unexpected and tangible way.

That gift of so long ago has continued to warm the Flowers family from one generation to the next as Charlie's son, my husband Charles, calls to mind each Christmas morning those two men and then whispers a prayer of remembrance and thanks. Charles never met them, yet they've had a lasting impact on his life.

Sharing our gratitude for God's blessings with others creates a chain of gratitude from one person to the next. Gratitude begets gratitude. It affects people in the present and people yet to be born. Our expressions of gratitude, our praises and thanksgiving, are the treasures we lay up in heaven, ". . . where moth and rust do not destroy, and where thieves do not break in and steal" (Matthew 6:20).

It might take some practice at first and some mental discipline, but anyone can develop a grateful heart. If it seems challenging, I believe that's because gratitude has been a neglected virtue in our culture. We have not given it the attention it deserves. Most of us have learned to be polite. We've learned to say thank you and please. But do these words come from our hearts? How many of us are genuinely grateful people? Perhaps our prayer, like that of Victor Herbert, should be, "Thou has given so much to me. Give one thing more—a grateful heart."[1]

MILES OF GRATEFULNESS

Brother David Steindl-Rast wrote in his book, *Gratefulness: The Heart of Prayer*, "Whatever causes us to look with amazement opens 'the eyes of our eyes.' We begin to see everything as a gift. An inch of surprise can lead to miles of gratefulness."[2]

I was surprised just days ago as I walked with my husband in a park by the San Diego Bay near our home. "Look at this place," I said, gazing from one scene to the next as though I were a first-time visitor. Water gently patted the sand. A flock of mud hens waddled across the grass. Kids pumped their swings high into the air. Old and young skaters whizzed by on roller blades. Gulls swooped and cawed in the distance as they searched for food.

Houses poked out of hills on the other side of the waterway. The morning sun broke up the clouds and filtered through giant eucalyptus trees along the path. My heart was full. Tears filled my eyes. What is happening to me? I wondered. I've been here hundreds of times. Why is it suddenly new and beautiful? Then I realized it was new because that day I recognized all these things as gifts!

"Thank you, Lord," I prayed, "for the opportunity to be here, to be alive, to walk and to talk, to see, feel and experience all of this." I kicked off my shoes and ran to the shoreline where I could walk barefoot in the cool sand. I stopped to listen to the birds overhead and gathered a few seashells to add to my collection.

What a wondrous experience I had that day. How different from other times when I had hurried to the park and back home just to get in my hour of exercise, oblivious to the sights and sounds around me; unaware that God made all this for me to enjoy. Like so many adults I had lost my sense of wonder and awe. I couldn't recognize God's gifts, so I couldn't receive them. Once we truly recognize the blessings that surround us and receive them as gifts, we can't contain ourselves! Like the psalmist we release our cry of praise and gratitude in prayer, in song and in writing. "Thank you, God!"

A BASKETFUL OF THANKS

It is up to each of us to choose gratefulness and then to express it. We can ask God to open our hearts to the gifts we may have overlooked and to guide us in expressing our thanksgiving and praise. We can do this every single day. Like me, you may benefit from the tangible help in this area that my husband and I received from a woman we met at Christmastime a number of years ago.

7

She introduced us to a practice that has inspired us to express our thanks in writing, as well as in prayer, every day. "If you want to be content, to experience peace," she said, "write down your blessings—the things you're grateful for—on slips of paper and put them in a container of some kind. A small basket or a box or bag will do. Soon it will be full to overflowing. From time to time look at what you wrote. No one can be discontent for long with so much to be thankful for."

Charles and I looked at each other and knew instantly that this was something we wanted to do. That year had been particularly stressful for us. Money was tight. We were so focused on what we were missing, it was hard to imagine what we might find to be grateful for, but we were willing. We had our faith. We had each other. We would start there and see what came next.

We found a silver foil gift bag in one of our closets, placed a label on the front that said "Our Blessing Bag," and set it on a table in our bedroom where it would be accessible night or day. And we made it easy to use by putting a small pad of paper and a pen beside it. As the new year began, we started recording our blessings. By November, just as the woman had promised, our container was "full to overflowing."

On Thanksgiving morning we propped ourselves up in bed and dumped the bag upside down on the quilt. It seemed a fitting day to review and give thanks for our many blessings—so many more than we ever would have noticed if we had not committed ourselves to writing them down and saving them.

"You go first," my husband said. So I grabbed one slip and read it aloud, then another and another. What a joy it was to read and experience these gifts all over again: a surprise visit from a dear friend my husband hadn't seen in over thirty years; a special walk 'n' talk we'd shared on the beach one morning topped off with hot tea and our favorite muffins; the safe arrival of a new grandchild; a wonderful mule pack trip in the Sierra Mountains; a new book contract; an old hurt healed through patience and prayer; a misunderstanding with a coworker cleared up. On and on I read. Then my husband grabbed a handful and continued.

By the time we got to the last scrap of paper we were in tears. How could we ever again doubt that God provides for our every need and protects our going out and coming in!

Notes

1. Frank S. Mead, ed., *The Encyclopedia of Religious Quotations* (Old Tappan, N. J.: Fleming Revell, 1965), 203.
2. Brother David Steindl-Rast, *Gratefulness, the Heart of Prayer* (New York: Paulist Press, 1984), 22.

Make It Personal

How to Use This Book

 YOU, TOO, can cultivate a more grateful heart. By using a Blessing Basket and the other tools in this book, you will experience a whole new awareness of God's faithfulness. A Blessing Basket is a tangible reminder to do more than merely think thankful thoughts. It is an invitation to go a step further: to create a habit, to write down the gifts—big and small—that come your way. Most of us go through life so eager to make things happen, to accumulate something for the future, to make our mark on the world that we nearly—and often completely—overlook or underestimate the blessings that are part of our lives.

Writing them down helps us hold on to them, to thank God for them and to share them with others. The next section of this book contains tools for cultivating a more grateful heart over forty days. Each day's activities are in four sections: a devotional reading, related Scripture verses to read and think about, questions for self-reflection and application, and a short prayer.

The daily readings are like "starter dough." As you begin to focus on what you have to be thankful for, at first you may have only a pinch of gratitude to offer the Lord. You may be so focused on the lack and loss in your life you cannot see the blessings. So begin where you are. God will meet you there. Before reading the pages for the day, ask the Lord to guide your thoughts and words toward Him. I think you'll be surprised at how the pinch of thanks you started with will expand until your entire being—like rising bread dough—overflows with praise.

After you've read the day's devotional, ponder the Scriptures that follow in the "Words to Reflect On" section. Each day includes a reading from the Psalms because King David's heart overflowed with gratitude. Reading a psalm a day is a wonderful way to cultivate the kind of thankfulness he demonstrated. As seventeenth-century English clergyman Jeremy Taylor reminds us, "Every furrow in the Book of Psalms is sown with seeds of thanksgiving."[1]

Then use the "Looking Within, Living It Out" questions to stimulate your thinking about how the day's reading relates to your life and what you have to be grateful for that day. Always end that time of reflection by writing down something to add to your Blessing Basket. The container itself is not important; it's what you put in it that counts. Over the years we've used flower or breadbaskets, gift bags or boxes, even a jar or two.

Finally, use the "Prayer Starter" to open a time set apart for thanking God and focusing your heart on His blessings. At the end of forty days, celebrate! Pour out the slips of paper in your Blessing Basket and read what you've written.

Once you've made counting your blessings a precious part of your daily routine, you need never again be at a loss for words of praise and thanksgiving to our gracious Lord, the One from whom all blessings flow! If you are married with children, invite your spouse and daughters and sons to participate in the Blessing Basket habit with you. Going through the book together and recording your blessings as a family is a satisfying and tangible way to promote family intimacy. If you don't have children, or if yours, like ours, are grown and gone, invite your husband or wife to join you in this adventure. Consider building it into your daily routine at a time when you are together—perhaps at the breakfast table each morning. The daily reading can lead to a fruitful discussion—much more edifying than trading stories about the day's news reports. If you prefer to add to your Blessing Basket in the evening, it can be a joyful way to close the day together before going to sleep.

If you live alone, you have the opportunity to make this an intensely personal experience. You may want to guard this time between you and the Lord and not allow anything to distract you. If you have roommates or live-in students or a prayer partner or spiritual mentor, you may wish to ask one or all to be part of this experience with you. Share this book with them and talk about how it can enrich each of you and your relationship as you go through it together.

Imagine the climate in a household where everyone participates in a commitment to cultivate a more grateful heart! Surely it would be "a taste of heaven."[2]

There is no one way to cultivate gratitude. Make it your journey, because if you don't feel comfortable and willing, you won't start. If members of your household don't share your enthusiasm, go forward without them. Don't let anyone or anything hinder you from cultivating your own grateful heart. My hunch is that within days of getting started, some of the stragglers may come running behind you, eager to catch up as they notice the changes in you and the benefits to them!

People who have practiced this simple daily exercise of thinking about what they're grateful for, recording it, and depositing their writings in a Blessing Basket, then reading them over at a later time, report wonderful results in their lives. They begin to notice changes in their experience of God, in their relationships at work, and with their spouse, their children and friends—even regarding pain and disappointment.

I pray that you, too, will be motivated to look at your life in a fresh way and to count it all good—the everyday gifts, great and small, the delightful as well as the disappointing, the lovely as well as the ugly, the predictable as well as the unpredictable—and to give thanks for each blessing in a new and deliberate way.

Notes

12

1. Mead, *The Encyclopedia of Religious Quotations*, 204.
2. William Romaine in Mead, *The Encyclopedia of Religious Quotations*, 204.

PART
TWO

FORTY DAILY
READINGS

Choosing Gratitude

 EVERY TIME we say thank you, we honor the Lord who made it possible. Every time we move out of our own small world and pay attention to the blessings—whether a comforting hand at a sickbed, a beautifully wrapped package at a birthday party, a smiling presence at a wedding or a comforting word at a graveside—we are emotionally and spiritually renewed.

As Nathaniel Parker Willis put it, "Gratitude is not only the memory, but the homage of the heart—rendered to God for His goodness."[1]

Developing the habit of giving thanks takes practice. First we must choose gratitude; then we will begin to see everything in our lives as a gift, regardless of the circumstances or the appearance. That doesn't mean we're expected to shout "Hallelujah!" when a loved one dies or if someone robs our home or if we're struck with a terminal illness. That wouldn't be human. But when we foster the habit of giving thanks in all things, as the apostle Paul counsels us in Colossians 3:17, we are able to see how God uses all these experiences for good. And for that we thank Him.

Losing our possessions in a flood or a fire can lead us away from materialism. Suffering from cancer may cause an independent person to lean on God for the first time ever. Divorce or the death of a spouse or friend may turn a heart toward Christ in a new way. Acquiring a habit is easier for some than for others.

Think about what it takes to lose weight or exercise regularly or spend quality time with our loved ones. A commitment to change takes conscious effort and repeated action. At first it sounds like work. It's daunting. We may feel afraid or overwhelmed. God understands. That is why He extends His grace for our every need. When we ask for His help, He opens our eyes to see life from His perspective.

Cultivating a heart of gratitude is not a contest or a race or a task; it's a way of life we choose to embrace. And as we do, the Lord promises to lead us: "I will lead the blind by ways they have not known, along unfamiliar paths I will guide them; I will turn the darkness into light before them and make the rough places smooth. These are the things I will do; I will not forsake them" (Isaiah 42:16).

One elderly man I know is still angry toward God over the unexpected death of his mother. Even now, forty years after the fact, he still lives without the comfort and love of God, the only one who can restore him. He admits he is lonely, afraid to leave his apartment, crippled with physical and emotional pain. Yet he will not let go. He has chosen bitterness over gratitude. He has made a habit of despair.

Richard Foster writes, "The decision to set the mind on the high things of life is an act of the will. It is not something that falls on our head."[2]

We must choose gratitude. Actor and comedian Bill Cosby exemplified this in a touching way at the graveside of his son,

Ennis, murdered in January 1997. "We now want to give praise to God for allowing us to know him," he said, "not for giving him to us, but just for letting us know him."[3]

Cosby's pain must have been almost unbearable as he watched his son's body lowered into the ground. Reporters scribbled their stories. Cameras flashed. Videotapes rolled. Bill Cosby could have been enraged, silent or distant, and no one would have blamed him. His only son—his "hero," as he often referred to him, lay dead in front of him at age twenty-seven. But Cosby chose, instead, to set his mind on a "higher thing"—on gratitude—to recognize that Ennis had been a gift, not a possession, not something he earned or deserved. And so he gave thanks. Will you?

WORDS TO REFLECT ON

Trust in the LORD and do good; dwell in the land and enjoy safe pasture. —PSALM 37:3

There is a time for everything, and a season for every
    activity under heaven:
a time to be born and a time to die,
a time to plant and a time to uproot,
a time to kill and a time to heal,
a time to tear down and a time to build,
a time to weep and a time to laugh,
a time to mourn and a time to dance,
a time to scatter stones and a time to gather them,
a time to embrace and a time to refrain,

a time to search and a time to give up,
a time to keep and a time to throw away,
a time to tear and a time to mend,
a time to be silent and a time to speak,
a time to love and a time to hate,
a time for war and a time for peace.

What does the worker gain from his toil? I have seen the burden God has laid on men. He has made everything beautiful in its time. He has also set eternity in the hearts of men; yet they cannot fathom what God has done from beginning to end. —ECCLESIASTES 3:1–11

18

LOOKING WITHIN, LIVING IT OUT

- Are you willing to choose gratitude? What will it cost you?
- What one thing can you do today to build the habit of giving thanks?
- Reflect on your relationships and identify one person who has made a significant impact on your life. Express your gratitude to him or her, either in person or in a letter.
- Write down the thing you are most grateful for about that person and drop it into your Blessing Basket.

PRAYER STARTER

Dear Lord, today I choose gratitude. I thank you for the gift of life–and death–and for everything in between: for sunrises and sunsets, for provision and loss, for laughter and tears, for joy and pain. I know there is a time for every purpose under heaven. I know that you will not withhold any good thing from me if I walk uprightly. Thank you that you are my God and I am your child and that I can depend on you as I seek the "high things" of life.

Notes

1. John P. Bradley, Leo F. Daniels, and Thomas C. Jones, comp., *The International Dictionary of Thoughts* (Chicago: J.C. Ferguson Publishing Co., 1969), 341.
2. Richard Foster, *Celebration of Discipline* (San Francisco: Harper and Row, 1978), 167.
3. Lawrie Mifflin, "Cosbys Want to Grieve With Dignity," *San Diego Union-Tribune*, January 28, 1997, A-4.

19

Welcoming Simple Pleasures

 AS THE FAMILIAR Shaker hymn reminds us, " 'Tis a gift to be simple, 'Tis a gift to be free. 'Tis a gift to come down where we ought to be."

Many of us must come down from our fantasy and grandiosity to reality before we can recognize the gift of simple things and the blessing of being free. One late afternoon after a long day of raking pine needles and pulling weeds with my husband at our weekend cabin in the mountains, I hobbled into the house, exhausted. Charles stayed behind to put away the gardening tools.

As I stepped into the shower, my mind started ticking off all the things left to do before our little hideaway would be just the way I wanted it. Wallpaper for the bathroom. New carpet for the living room and bedroom. Pretty curtains for the windows. And it would be nice to buy a new sofa bed and a matching chair and some kitchen dishes and pictures for the walls and . . . A hard rap on the bathroom window jarred me out of my fantasy. There stood Charles smiling at me, his face smudged, his eyes bright.

"What's up?" I called over the pelting water.

"Not much," he answered. "I miss you, that's all. The sun's almost down," he added gently, pointing toward the mountains, "and I want you here beside me as the day ends."

A little shiver ran down my spine. Here was a gesture so simple, a gift so lovely, it took my breath away and brought me down to where I ought to be. What did it matter, in that moment, that we didn't have everything in place? We had each other. We had this day. We had the simple pleasure of watching, arm in arm, the golden sun slip behind the hills.

How cleansing it would be if we were all to welcome more simple pleasures into our lives and then give thanks for the freedom they bring. Simplicity can restore a sense of dignity, purpose and balance. Perhaps we turn from simplicity because we mistake it for austerity. But it is not the same thing at all! Austerity renounces the things of the world; simplicity puts them in perspective.

Simplicity encourages us to be well, look well, feel well and do well without making a statement about it. By coming down to where we ought to be—content and grateful—we find we need less, want less, have less and do less. Like the apostle Paul, we can be content in plenty or in want. And when we are content with simple things, we have more room in our hearts for appreciation and gratitude.

WORDS TO REFLECT ON

Blessed are those who have learned to acclaim you, who walk in the light of your presence, O LORD. They rejoice in your name all day long; they exult in your righteousness. —PSALM 89:15, 16

I delight greatly in the LORD; my soul rejoices in my God. For he has clothed me with garments of salvation and arrayed me in a robe of righteousness, as a bridegroom adorns his head like a priest, and as a bride adorns herself with her jewels. —ISAIAH 61:10

I have told you this so that my joy may be in you and that your joy may be complete. —JOHN 15:11

LOOKING WITHIN, LIVING IT OUT

- In what ways do you need to "come down" to where you ought to be?
- What are some of the simple things in your life that you may not have welcomed as gifts?
- How can you simplify your life in order to experience more contentment and gratitude?
- Write down five simple gifts you are thankful for and drop them into your Blessing Basket.

PRAYER STARTER

God, thank you for the gift of simple pleasures: sunrises, sunsets, birds singing in the tree outside my window, children laughing, an old man and woman walking hand-in-hand through the park, a baby's smile, homemade soup on a cold night, huddling with friends around a bright campfire, riding a horse on the beach, catching a wave, making angels in the snow. Today I choose to come down to where I ought to be—with you right here and now, simple and free.

Appreciating Life

AS THE EARTH rumbled and stirred, Robert Girt, in his apartment on Sixteenth Avenue in Anchorage, Alaska, dropped the shoes he was polishing. "It's a quake," he said half aloud.

In another part of town, J. D. Peters walked out to meet his wife as she pulled into the driveway of their home. All at once the ground shook, then gave way.

"Come on, Honey!" Peters yelled to his wife. But as he stretched out his hand toward her, the driveway opened between them. They faced each other across a gaping hole.

Peters ran to the garage and grabbed an extension cord. He tried to throw it to his wife, but it wouldn't reach. And before he could think what to do next, his house reared like an angry mule and slid toward the sea. "Hang on!" Peters shouted. Next, as suddenly as it had opened, the giant gap closed, and his wife slid across to him.

Meanwhile, young Robert Girt had no time to think about his half-polished shoes. He and his father began leading the two younger children out of the apartment. Just then everything went to pieces. Plaster fell and the building swayed back and forth violently.

Quickly, Girt's family rushed down the fire escape and into the street. Then Robert fought his way back into the building. First, he dragged a woman to safety. Next, he rammed into a locked apartment and saved an eighty-three-year-old man. And finally, choking and gasping for breath, he smashed through jammed doors, saving a screaming woman and another elderly man. Then, at last, he rescued his sister's cat, cowering in a closet.

By the next day, Robert Girt, safe with his family, could once again give some thought to polishing his shoes. And the Peters were safe and grateful to be alive, even though they had lost their home and Mr. Peters had broken three ribs.

This earthquake occurred in 1964, yet a similar scenario has taken place in cities and countries around the world throughout history. During a recent fire in southern California, for example, neighbors saved a family's home with garden hoses. A newspaper the following morning published a picture of the rescued house displaying a large banner that said THANK YOU to friends and neighbors.

Whenever disaster strikes, people's lives change suddenly. At first, many victims of fire or avalanche or earthquake or accident feel God is punishing them or singling them out from the rest. Most feel overwhelmed with a sense of guilt, fear and aloneness. Others rise up and act in unusual ways during a disaster. Quiet people turn into heroes, like Robert Girt, rescuing children and animals from danger. Talkative people may become scared and shy. And adults may find they are as much in need of comfort as their children.

Survivors are often so upset they can't fully understand what has happened. Some stare at their surroundings in silence. Others

25

panic. But after a while, even though death and destruction are all around, most disaster victims are simply glad to be alive. They want to get on with their lives. Together they work to repair their homes, businesses and property. And as strangers become friends, they remember their need for each other. Most appreciate life more. They learn the value of family and friends, and they become grateful in a way they never considered before.

WORDS TO REFLECT ON

I will not violate my covenant or alter what my lips have uttered. —PSALM 89:34

But I will rescue you on that day, declares the LORD; you will not be handed over to those you fear. I will save you; you will not fall by the sword but will escape with your life, because you trust in me, declares the LORD. —JEREMIAH 39:17, 18

Have no fear of sudden disaster or of the ruin that overtakes the wicked, for the LORD will be your confidence and will keep your foot from being snared. —PROVERBS 3:25, 26

LOOKING WITHIN, LIVING IT OUT

- How have you used a crisis or tragedy in your life as an excuse to stop praising and thanking God?

- In what specific way can you embrace the gift of life today?
- With whom can you share your appreciation of life? Who needs to hear your grateful perspective?
- Write down the thing you are most grateful for regarding the gift of life and drop it in your Blessing Basket.

PRAYER STARTER

Faithful God, today I embrace and thank you for the gift of life. When I read about the devastating effects of natural disasters on the lives of people all over the world, I am awakened to how blessed I've been, how generous you have been toward me. I promise today to turn my heart toward gratitude and to share myself more fully with the people in my life. Let me see these gifts now— today—not only when faced with a crisis.

27

Celebrating Friendships

 MOST OF US can point to an event or experience that has made us aware of the importance of giving thanks for special people. These occasions remind us that expressing gratitude is one of the most simple, yet most profound, ways we can display our recognition of one of God's most precious gifts: the gift of friendship.

Weddings and births are among the most special occasions to express our gratitude for friends. Even funerals provide an opportunity to give thanks. Grief and gratitude mingle as we suffer the loss of someone we love, but, at the same time, offer thanks for life and the time we shared together.

Birthdays, christenings, anniversaries, holidays and victory celebrations are opportunities to give thanks for loved ones. There are other times, too, that may be less important by society's standards, but they are times that provide special opportunities to give thanks through our actions:

- visiting the sick and the terminally ill,
- sharing a friend's grief over loss,
- going to court with a loved one on the day of a final divorce decree.

How many of us have considered such actions expressions of gratitude? Yet they are. Being there in person during these times communicates care, concern and appreciation.

Your presence says, "You matter. I am grateful for you." When we express our gratitude for others, important things happen to them and to us. We renew our friendship and love. We restore ourselves emotionally and spiritually. And we learn how much we really mean to each other.

Ken Miller made this discovery through his friends shortly before he died. Some years ago Ken worked as a consultant for my husband, Charles, in a large medical facility in Los Angeles. The year Ken turned seventy-five, Charles and others decided to plan a surprise dinner party for him in honor of his birthday and as a way of saying "thank you" for all he had contributed during his fifty years of service. However, as Charles began compiling the guest list with help from some of Ken's friends, he realized what had started as a simple, unassuming evening was turning into an occasion of great significance. The names given him were men of prestige, presidents of corporations, leaders in industry and manufacturing.

When Charles ushered Ken into the banquet room of the hotel on the night of the party, eighteen of the most prominent men in the Los Angeles community surrounded them. At once they all rose to their feet in celebration of this outstanding individual who was responsible for much of their success and fortune. Each one seemed to know that the only way to attempt to thank Ken was to be there in person on this grand occasion.

Throughout the evening Ken sat nearly speechless, in awe of what was going on around him, as one by one each man stood before him and shared his gratitude as a personal tribute. Ken told my husband that no plaque or promotion or pomp and ceremony could have had more meaning. This man who had made such an impact on so many carried that event in his heart till the day he died.

WORDS TO REFLECT ON

Rejoice in the LORD, you who are righteous, and praise his holy name. —PSALM 97:12

Dear children, let us not love with words or tongue but with actions and in truth. —1 JOHN 3:18

Be devoted to one another in brotherly love. Honor one another above yourselves. —ROMANS 12:10

LOOKING WITHIN, LIVING IT OUT

- How have people in your life shown their gratitude for you through friendship?
- In what tangible way can you demonstrate your gratitude for someone's friendship?
- What emotional and spiritual gifts have you received through this friendship?
- Make a list of friends you are grateful for and why. Drop it into your Blessing Basket.

PRAYER STARTER

Dear God, thank you for the gift of friends. They've been with me when I've cried, stood by me through illness and disappointment, held me up during the death of loved ones, shared my wonder at the birth of my children, and celebrated with me when I acquired my degree or landed a promotion at work. Most of all, I thank you for friends who have walked with me in spirit and in faith, upholding me, exhorting me, confiding in me and sharing with me the joy of our relationship in Christ.

31

Noticing God's Presence

NO MATTER HOW much we love God or how well we know Him, there is always more to know and love, to recognize and receive, to notice and be grateful for. Even David, as close as he was to the Lord, yearned for more: "My soul thirsts for God, for the living God" (Psalm 42:2).

His presence and His power are reflected everywhere we look—in a delicate flower, in the raging sea, in a trickling stream, on a majestic peak—in people, places and things. We are never without His comforting arm, His encouraging Word, His close and watchful eye. "I will instruct you and teach you in the way you should go; I will counsel you and watch over you" (Psalm 32:8).

If we go to the bottom of the sea, He is there. If we go to the top of a mountain, He is there. He is with us as we draw our first breath and beside us as we breathe our last. He is the beginning, the end, the author and the finisher of all things. How could our lives be anything but a hymn of grateful praise?

In the summer of 1988, as I hiked to the top of Half Dome Mountain during a women's backpacking trip to Yosemite National Park, I had an experience that forever changed the way I view God's presence. This was a trip I had wanted to take for years so I had planned every detail months in advance. I hiked weekly with a group of friends to build up my endurance, learned about tents and sleeping bags, boots and stoves, and dehydrated food.

On the morning of our ascent I awoke early, excited, nervous, eager to get started. I wanted to experience it fully, with no regrets. I knew it was up to me to make it happen, to create a memory I would not forget. So halfway up the steep rock face, I did something I never thought I could do. I stopped, turned around and stood facing out.

There was no room for a false step so I held onto the cable for support. Then I took a deep breath and looked! In front of me and to the sides, up, down—everywhere I gazed was a visual feast of massive pines hovering over giant cliffs, powerful boulders poised among lush greenery, and majestic peaks jutting into the deep blue sky. I could scarcely take it in. It was so much more than I had expected. I thought to myself, *This is a holy place. God is here.* Because the physical details of the trip had taken a lot of my attention, I had not thought much about the spiritual impact it might have, but here it was.

"Oh God," I prayed, "thank you for your presence here—in the trees and peaks and boulders, waterfalls and flowers. Everything I need and want—physically and spiritually—is right here with you."

Cool water from a rushing stream quenched my thirst, revived my spirit as well as my parched skin, and when boiled, turned dehydrated food into delicious soup. Fire under my miniature stove heated my food, warmed my feet and comforted my soul on a chilly evening. And the stars and moon put on a bountiful show each night before I fell asleep.

33

I didn't need lovely clothes, a new car, theater tickets or a gourmet meal. What I needed I could carry. What I couldn't carry, God provided: a cluster of boulders and rocks and a few sturdy tree limbs were all the furniture I required; a bed of pine needles made a comfortable carpet for my tent; a broad old tree provided stumps for seats; limbs for hanging wet socks; and branches for shade. Hours and hours of time to reflect quietly and to pray gave me an entirely new perspective on my life, both there in the mountains and back home. God was here with me—in this wild place—meeting my every need and desire. How could I not notice His presence?

WORDS TO REFLECT ON

He will be like rain falling on a mown field, like showers watering the earth. In his days the righteous will flourish; prosperity will abound till the moon is no more. He will rule from sea to sea and from the River to the ends of the earth. The desert tribes will bow before him and his enemies will lick the dust. —PSALM 72:6–9

Sing for joy, O heavens, for the LORD has done this; shout aloud, O earth beneath. Burst into song, you mountains, you forests and all your trees, for the LORD has redeemed Jacob, he displays his glory in Israel. —ISAIAH 44:23

Do not be afraid, little flock, for your Father has been pleased to give you the kingdom. —LUKE 12:32

LOOKING WITHIN, LIVING IT OUT

- In what ways have you enjoyed the gift of God's creation without acknowledging and giving thanks for His presence in it?
- As you go about your day today, watch for God's presence and thank Him for what you see.
- As you reflect on God's creation, in what gift of nature do you most notice Him?
- Consider that gift—flower, tree, water, bird—and write down your words of gratitude. Add them to your Blessing Basket.

PRAYER STARTER

Dear God, I can no longer be complacent about your gifts. Everywhere I look I notice your presence. Today I thank you for the flowers that poke out of the ground after a spring rain, for the clouds overhead and the wind in the trees, for the mountains and rivers, and streams in the desert. How shortsighted I have been! You are higher, deeper, broader and stronger than any mountain or sea or valley or meadow. But still these things reflect your glory and turn my heart toward gratitude. Open my eyes to see all this—and more.

Giving and Receiving Gifts of the Heart

 WE CAN ALL remember times in our lives when God has given us a gift so unexpected and so delightful, we are speechless. We couldn't have planned or anticipated it. Lois had just such an experience.

Thanks to a group of smiling, brown-faced *niños* who gave from their hearts, she learned how to receive in a new and deeper way. It all started one hot, dusty Saturday in 1986 as her church van pulled into the dirt parking lot in front of a group of worn wooden buildings and scattered lean-tos known as Orfanatorio El Sauzel in Ensenada, Mexico.

"Hola! Como esta usted? Como se llama?" She rehearsed the new phrases nervously under her breath as the van doors opened to a cluster of boys and girls aged two to fifteen. To the side stood a quiet little one named Veronica.

"Her shy, serious eyes and the soft sprinkling of freckles across her nose caught my attention," Lois says.

Then there was Charo, a plump and pretty ten-year-old who quickly grabbed her hand and pulled her away from the crowd to look at a newborn puppy. In an instant, Lois' discomfort disappeared.

"I realized I didn't need Spanish. The barrier of language and culture dissolved as we skipped across the yard together." The day passed much too quickly. Finger games, yarn dolls, books and songs filled the hours. "There were lots of hugs and kisses and lap stories, too. Before I knew it, it was time to say *adios*."

As the van wound through the mountain roads toward the U.S. border, Lois leaned against the dusty window. I haven't felt this great in years, she thought. She was also grimy, sticky and exhausted, but that didn't matter. What made this day so special? Lois wondered. Seeing and meeting those sweet children, of course, but it was more than that.

"It was the preciousness of people really being with each other," she explains. "They couldn't rely on idle conversation or the clutter of stuff. And no one cared about my college degree or where I lived or how much money I had."

Lois says the best thing about the day was just being herself and enjoying the freedom to experience the joy and spontaneity of the children. The boys and girls lived amidst poverty, yet they made her feel rich. "They had nothing to give but themselves," she says. "I learned so much from them. They grabbed our hands, climbed into our laps, wrapped their arms around our necks, and smiled with eyes and hearts that left me limp with emotion. I was overwhelmed with gratitude: for the children, for the opportunity, for just being there."

Lois says the experience challenged her to bring more of her real self to every relationship in her life. "I don't have time for superficial conversations or meaningless get-togethers. When I saw how God used those orphan children to bless me, to show me who I really am, I knew I would never be the same again."

WORDS TO REFLECT ON

Blessed is the man who does not walk in the counsel of the wicked or stand in the way of sinners or sit in the seat of mockers . . . He is like a tree planted by streams of water, which yields its fruit in season and whose leaf does not wither. Whatever he does prospers. —PSALM 1:1, 3

If you spend yourselves in behalf of the hungry and satisfy the needs of the oppressed, then your light will rise in the darkness, and your night will become like the noonday. —ISAIAH 58:10

Jesus looked at him and loved him. "One thing you lack," he said. "Go, sell everything you have and give to the poor, and you will have treasure in heaven. Then come, follow me." —MARK 10:21

LOOKING WITHIN, LIVING IT OUT

- Has another person ever blessed you with a gift of the heart? How did you receive it?
- Have you ever given a gift of the heart to someone else? What response did you receive?
- How might you "spend" yourself today from the heart?
- Write down a gift of the heart you've received and add it to your Blessing Basket.

PRAYER STARTER

Dear God, thank you for gifts of the heart. Thank you for showing me what really matters is relationships—first with you and then with others. I want to spend more time with my loved ones, cuddle the children in my life, read to an elderly neighbor, listen attentively to someone who needs to talk. Thank you for opportunities to bless others with my presence and to receive the blessing of their presence in return.

Hoping in Christ

 IT IS GOOD and right we thank God for family and friends and work and possessions, for the earth and sea and sky. But without Christ, none of it would matter much over the span of our lives. It is our hope in Him that forms the ground on which we stand—the ground of gratitude for life, now and forever.

For years, I was ground in false hope, and I paid a high price. I *hoped* my marriage would work out. I *hoped* we'd have enough money to buy a new home. I "hoped" my son and daughters would be healthy and happy. I *hoped* I'd become a published writer. And I tied myself to a slavish routine of activities I *hoped* would bring all this about.

I read books on marriage, looked at new homes and learned about real estate. I began shopping for healthier foods and added vitamins to my grocery list. I took courses in writing and attended publishing conferences. I became lost in *hope*. Deep inside I remained hopeless.

Then some fifteen years later I experienced something that changed the way I look at hope and gratitude. It started the day

I opened the door to Dr. Brady's suite, shaking with apprehension. I hope this works, I told myself sternly. It had taken all my courage to make this counseling appointment. Get in, get a few tips and get out, I whispered to myself. I honestly believed the solution to my problems could fit on a Post-it note.

Within minutes, Dr. Brady ushered me into his office. "Tell me, what has brought you here?" he asked. I took a deep breath, rushed through the chronology of events that had led to our meeting—my husband's interest in another woman and our mounting debt—then sat back and waited for a solution.

Dr. Brady pulled his chair forward. "I don't have the answer," he said, "but there is one, and I feel certain you'll discover it as we work together." As I continued seeing Dr. Brady, he asked about my spiritual life and what I knew about God. I didn't see what any of this had to do with my troubled marriage, but over time he showed me the hole in my soul had been there all along—long before I married my husband.

I had grown up in a legalistic church. It seemed to me rules were more important than relationships. If someone told me what to do, I did it. Now, in my marriage, I expected that same formula to work. But it didn't. My problems were too big for a pat answer. I stopped counseling after two years, thanked Dr. Brady for pointing me in the right direction, and embarked on a path that took me through every kind of church service and spiritual seminar that came my way.

I read books, listened to tapes, prayed the best way I knew how, and attended a Bible study. I remember how the message in the Gospel of John struck me about Jesus Christ being the Son of God.

One chilly Tuesday morning in December 1982 as I was returning home from a walk along the beach, I came to the end of myself. Nothing made sense anymore. I sat down where I was and sobbed. "God," I cried out, "who are you? Do you care anything about me? I feel hopeless. I've tried to find you. I want to know you."

Seconds passed. Then, ever so gently, a stream of familiar words came to mind: "I am the way and the truth and the life. No one comes to the Father except through me." I had read these words of Jesus Christ in John 14:6 dozens of times. Why did they sound so different now? I wondered. Then I knew. I had never let them sink in before. I had never heard them for myself. That winter day I did hear them—*for me*. I jumped up.

"Jesus Christ is the way to God!" I shouted to the waves and to the sky. And to think I almost missed Him! Here was the hope I had been looking for. No higher power, life force or spiritual guide had offered me such assurance. "O God, thank you for your Son, Jesus," I whispered.

Everything was new in that moment. I was no longer a victim of my husband's actions against me. All have sinned and all fall short of the glory of God. That included me. I had known that from Paul's teaching (Romans 3:23), but until that day I had never taken it to heart. No wonder I had not fully received this gift before. I had not seen myself as a sinner because I was too preoccupied with the sins others had committed against me.

But that day I knew I needed forgiveness as much as anyone else. How grateful I was to know from my own experience that Christ did not come for the righteous, but for sinners to repent (Matthew 9:13). I was a sinner, and I prayed that day for forgiveness as I put my hope and trust in Christ as my Savior. I began my new life that day.

My challenges did not clear up overnight. My husband left and did not come back. More importantly, I discovered peace and gratitude in a way I had not known before. I was absolutely certain I could survive and triumph over anything life brought my way as long as my hope was in Christ Jesus. And that has proven true ever since.

WORDS TO REFLECT ON

Be strong and take heart, all you who hope in the LORD. —PSALM 31:24

Praise be to the God and Father of our Lord Jesus Christ! In his great mercy he has given us new birth into a living hope through the resurrection of Jesus Christ from the dead. —1 PETER 1:3

To them God has chosen to make known among the Gentiles the glorious riches of this mystery, which is Christ in you, the hope of glory. —COLOSSIANS 1:27

LOOKING WITHIN, LIVING IT OUT

- In what ways have you depended on the hope of the world instead of on the hope God offers through Jesus Christ?
- What has Christ done for you to awaken your hope in Him?
- How can you share that hope with others so they might turn their hearts to Him in gratitude?
- Write down a gift in your life that exemplifies your hope in Christ and add it to your Blessing Basket.

PRAYER STARTER

Oh God, I thank you for the hope I have in Jesus Christ, my Savior and Lord. Thank you that I can rest in this truth, no longer searching in vain for the things I long for. Everything begins and ends with you. I am grateful and I praise you for your mercy and kindness to me, a sinner. You have rescued me from the world, restored me from my destructive ways, and given me real hope through my new life in Christ.

"Being There"

SHOWING OUR gratitude for others is no small thing. It is not simply a polite gesture, such as applauding after a performance or giving a large tip. Often it requires going out of our way, giving our presence in support and appreciation.

In ancient Jewish culture people considered it a solemn duty to respond affirmatively to a wedding invitation, a burial ceremony or other momentous occasion. They would have thought it an insult to make an excuse or to beg off once invited. Everyone knew what it took to prepare for such an event: Fatted calves butchered, fine linens set out, musicians hired to play for the guests, and only the finest food and wines served.

Centuries later the first settlers in America demonstrated a similar spirit. The Pilgrims set such store by their belief in the freedom to worship together that they risked their lives and fortunes to seek community on a distant shore. One of their first public displays after arriving in the new land was a feast of thanksgiving.

As our country expanded and grew, it was not uncommon for an entire town to turn out to witness a baby's christening, celebrate the union of a young woman with her betrothed, honor a brave soldier, raise a barn, harvest a crop or put out a fire. The first Americans knew how to express their gratitude using more than words; they came running from near and far to be with one another.

Today some people are disinterested in the suffering and celebrations of neighbors and friends. To ignore these experiences, however, is to diminish one of the fundamental needs of society: to support each other individually and collectively, in times of victory and in times of defeat.

It is critical to make time to express gratitude together. So what if we're tired or busy? We have only this moment to act before it slips away forever. Sometimes we have to go out of our way—as my friend Angela did for me several years ago.

She spotted me across the lawn at my daughter's wedding reception. Much joy and pain and bitterness had passed between us over the course of our relationship. We had allowed a terrible misunderstanding to keep us apart for years. Then after my divorce, my move to a new city and my eventual remarriage, we experienced another long separation.

But that day, as our eyes met, we darted between clusters of guests and rushed into a tight embrace. "Thank you for coming," I said, surprised at the deep gratitude I felt for her.

Angela whispered back "I've missed you" with such emotion, I nearly cried.

Conversation was unnecessary as we hugged one another. Her presence was a gift I had not expected, and the fact we hadn't seen each other in a long time made it even more special. She was older, as was I, but also more mellow, wise and seasoned by the suffering and joy she'd experienced in life.

That night I jotted down a single line on a small square of paper: Thank you for Angela. As I dropped it into my Blessing Basket, I offered a prayer of thanks to the One who taught us to show our gratitude for—and with—each other.

WORDS TO REFLECT ON

I will praise the LORD, who counsels me; even at night my heart instructs me. —PSALM 16:7

Nehemiah said, "Go and enjoy choice food and sweet drinks, and send some to those who have nothing prepared. This day is sacred to our Lord. Do not grieve, for the joy of the LORD is your strength." —NEHEMIAH 8:10

Whoever loves his brother lives in the light, and there is nothing in him to make him stumble. —1 JOHN 2:10

47

LOOKING WITHIN, LIVING IT OUT

- How have you responded to others during the momentous occasions of their lives? Have you expressed your gratitude by "being there," or have you fallen back on mere gestures?
- What action could you take today to demonstrate "being there" for one of your loved ones?

- How might you "be there" for someone outside your circle of family and close friends? (For example, bring dinner to an ailing neighbor, drive an elderly person to an appointment, and visit the sick in a nursing home.)
- List some of the people in your life who have shown their gratitude for you by sharing in your joys and sorrows. Drop their names into your Blessing Basket.

PRAYER STARTER

Lord God, thank you for showing me that thanking others is more than a gesture. Sometimes I need to go out of my way to make my gratitude known by "being there" during the momentous occasions of others' lives. Help me to know when I need to say thank you in person instead of sending flowers or a note or a card or making a phone call.

Involving Yourself

SOMETIMES SAYING thank you takes a public form. You go out of your home, sometimes out on a limb. You push beyond your comfortable limits and put yourself in a situation that may involve risk. Instead of writing a check or donating blankets and canned goods to a relief fund, you take yourself to the needy and bring your resources in person.

Louise and Kevin, a couple in our community, did just that for a number of years. They visited a homeless shelter each month and shared gifts of food, toys, clothes, time and love. They organized a game of softball one minute and held toddlers in their arms the next. "We have so much to be grateful for," Louise explains. "This is our way of saying thank you."

Some people express their gratitude by bringing people in need into their homes and hearts. Les and Roberta adopted two young children and then three more children all at once—a year or two later. The parents of the three had died in an accident, and the placement agency didn't want to split up the remaining family, so the couple took them all.

"We've been blessed," says Roberta. "Look at our life. How could we not share it?"

Beth and her husband, Bill, had a similar experience. When they realized they couldn't have children of their own, they decided to adopt a son with special needs. A year later they adopted two daughters. Now they're a thriving family sharing a big country farmhouse in Pennsylvania.

"We have a lot to be thankful for," Beth says. "These children needed parents and a home, and we wanted a family."

As I reflect on what Louise and Kevin, Les and Roberta, and Bill and Beth have done, I'm in awe of their generosity. Like me, you may be wondering if you have what it takes to involve yourself in the lives of others in such a permanent way.

A permanent commitment, however, may not always be called for. Our cities are full with opportunities to reach out to those in need. Local hospitals have babies to cuddle and sick children to visit and play with. Homeless shelters need tutors and readers. Nursing homes are open to friends and neighbors willing to lead a song, play the piano, hold a hand or share a memory.

Foreign student programs need people to house visiting students for a few weeks or months. These experiences remind us in significant and sometimes in ordinary ways that we really are our brother's keeper and that giving thanks in word and action is part of the ancient commandment, "Love your neighbor as yourself" (Leviticus 19:18).

WORDS TO REFLECT ON

He has scattered abroad his gifts to the poor, his right-eousness endures forever; his horn will be lifted high in honor. —PSALM 112:9

For I was hungry and you gave me something to eat, I was thirsty and you gave me something to drink, I was a stranger and you invited me in, I needed clothes and you clothed me, I was sick and you looked after me, I was in prison and you came to visit me. —MATTHEW 25:35, 36

Each one should use whatever gift he has received to serve others, faithfully administering God's grace in its various forms. —1 PETER 4:10

LOOKING WITHIN, LIVING IT OUT

- What resources do you have that you could share with others?
- In what ways have you expressed your thanks to God by involving yourself in the lives of those in need?
- What specific steps could you take today to share the gifts God has given you?
- List three ways people have been kind to you. How has their kindness made you more grateful? Add your list to your Blessing Basket.

PRAYER STARTER

Dear God, you have given me so much. Today I want to express my gratitude for these gifts by putting myself into your world. There are children to feed and clothe, older people to talk to and pray with, men and women living on the streets, single mothers trying to raise children without a father in their home. Lord, I thank you for these opportunities to share with others the gifts of love and provision you have given to me.

52

Grieving with Gratitude

"**I'VE ALWAYS** admired you," the woman wrote, "but now I admire you even more. I've been watching you grieve with grace."

Bonnie received this note of encouragement from a woman in her church on the first anniversary of the death of Bonnie's husband, Warren. Tears came to her eyes as she shared the letter with me one evening. I got teary-eyed too.

The woman was right. When Bonnie lost her husband of forty years, she hadn't let her grief consume her. She'd let herself be human, allowing those of us who know and love her to see the pain and the deep loss she felt, but she never burdened us with it. She grieved with grace, leaning on God to sustain her moment by moment.

It was not the first time. In 1968 Bonnie's nine-year-old daughter, Pam, lay packed in ice in the intensive care unit. In the five days following heart surgery, Pam's heart had stopped twice, and her brain was no longer functioning. "The doctor told us that if she survived, she'd live in a vegetative state," Bonnie says. For days before, during and after the surgery, Bonnie prayed her daughter would be a happy, healthy little girl with a strong heart.

One evening, however, it became clear she needed to release Pam. "As my husband and I drove home from the hospital we talked about it. Finally, I thanked God for her life and returned her to Him. We had been home only a short time when we received a call from the hospital. Pam had died. In the days that followed, through terrible grief, I realized if my child could not be with me, there was no other place I'd want her to be than with her heavenly Father. So in gratitude, I thanked Him for taking her home."

Bonnie admits that none of this came easily; her grief was wrenching. Deep in her heart, she knew God was loving and caring for Pam beyond anything she could imagine. When Warren died during a game of tennis twenty-seven years later, grief struck Bonnie again. The husband, partner, lover and friend she had cherished was suddenly gone. Yet in the midst of her grief and deep loneliness she discovered it was gratitude that lifted her once again.

"There is nothing I could want more for Warren than to be with his Lord and Savior," she says. "My days are lonely without the two I loved so much, but how grateful I am for each of them, for the joy they have now, and for the assurance that one day I will be with them again."

WORDS TO REFLECT ON

My flesh and my heart may fail, but God is the strength of my heart and my portion forever. —PSALM 73:26

He will swallow up death forever. The Sovereign LORD will wipe away the tears from all faces; he will remove the disgrace of his people from all the earth. The LORD has spoken. —ISAIAH 25:8

For just as the sufferings of Christ flow over into our lives, so also through Christ our comfort overflows. —2 CORINTHIANS 1:5

55

LOOKING WITHIN, LIVING IT OUT

- What are some of the major losses in your life? Does your grief include gratitude for the gifts you have lost?
- Have you grieved with grace, or are you angry because things did not go according to your plan?
- Write your own psalm expressing your grief over your loss and giving thanks for God's gift to you.
- Write down some things you are grateful for as a result of a loss you've suffered. Add them to your Blessing Basket.

PRAYER STARTER

Lord, thank you for the people I've known who have gone on to be with you. I did nothing to earn or deserve them. I know they were gifts from you, and I praise you for being so generous. I know it's natural and human to miss loved ones, but today I want to focus on gratitude for their lives, instead of grief over their deaths. You have blessed me with these dear ones for the time you allowed, and I thank you for the way each one has enriched my life.

Embracing Hidden Blessings

SOMETIMES IT takes seeing others suffer to awaken us to how blessed we are. It's as though God catches us by the sleeve and says, "Look across the street, down the road, over the hill. You can learn from those folks: They know what pain is. They know what it means to be disappointed and yet they praise me."

I had such an experience when I was a young mother. One evening I set out for a nearby mall for some time alone—to shop, to think, to enjoy the cool night air. On the walkway in front of my favorite department store a young woman sat in a wheelchair. Two little girls stood beside her. She had a tiny, deformed frame, shiny blond hair and gnarled hands that looked lifeless in her lap. I shivered, wondering what it would be like to be so restricted.

I continued past them into the store. Later, on the way back to my car, I was startled to see them still there.

"Is anything wrong?" I asked.

Nothing could have prepared me for the woman's speech. Each syllable a separate battle, she gulped and searched carefully for words.

"We ordered a cab nearly two hours ago and it hasn't come." Then she reached out for my hand. "Thank you for stopping. People usually don't."

I didn't admit that I'd hesitated. I had wanted that evening all to myself.

"I can do most things other women can even though I'm in this chair." She patted it lovingly. "It just takes me a little longer. And I have my daughters," she added, reaching out for them. "They help me. I have a lot to be thankful for."

My eyes filled with tears. I felt ashamed of the selfish thoughts that had enslaved me all evening. I had been eager to get away from my blessings: my kids, my husband, my dog, my home. She, on the other hand, considered even her wheelchair a gift. I had a lot to learn, and she was teaching me, whether she realized it or not.

"Why don't I drive you home?" I asked. "Where do you live?"

"Over there," the older girl said, pointing to an apartment complex about a half mile away.

"That's not far," I said. "Let's go." I motioned in the direction of my car.

The girls wheeled their mother to my car and helped her get in. Then they collapsed the wheelchair and put it into the trunk. They were obviously experienced. I watched in awe.

I introduced myself and the girls' mother did the same.

"I'm Katie," she said, "and these are my daughters, Lisa and Laurie."

A few minutes later we pulled up to their apartment building, and brown-eyed Laurie said, "We can make it from here. Thanks for the ride."

"Thank you!" I called after them.

I drove home, eager to hug and kiss my husband and children, pet the dog, and embrace my life. Pain! What did I know about pain? Not much, when I compared my life to Katie's. But she didn't focus on what she didn't have; rather, she embraced what she did have. She recognized her blessings, easily overlooked by others, and gave thanks.

WORDS TO REFLECT ON

You are my hiding place; you will protect me from trouble and surround me with songs of deliverance. —PSALM 32:7

Do not gloat over me, my enemy! Though I have fallen, I will rise. Though I sit in darkness, the LORD will be my light. —MICAH 7:8

In this world you will have trouble. But take heart! I have overcome the world. —JOHN 16:33

LOOKING WITHIN, LIVING IT OUT

- What happens to you when you focus on your pain instead of on the blessings behind it?
- What might God be trying to teach you through your pain? What hidden blessing can you find and embrace?

- How have you responded to the pain of other people? Are you a blessing or a greater burden?
- Write down one of the blessings God has revealed to you through a painful trial in your life and add it to your Blessing Basket.

PRAYER STARTER

Oh God, how shortsighted I am sometimes. I look at my problems and stop there, instead of looking behind and beyond them for the gifts you have for me. You say in your Word that all things work together for good, but I forget that promise when I focus on my hurt. Today I want to thank you for the blessings hidden among the pain. Help me to embrace both.

Thanking God in Faith

 JESUS PROMISED His disciples that if they had faith they would have power with God and with men. In the New Testament the Hebrews author reminds believers, "Faith is being sure of what we hope for and certain of what we do not see" (Hebrews 11:1).

Faith recognizes God's gifts before we see or receive them. David met Goliath believing that God would deliver the Philistine into his hands. God did. And David praised Him. The woman with the hemorrhage touched Jesus' garment, believing He would heal her, and her faith made her well. Imagine the gratitude she must have felt!

A few years ago I had my own experience of being sure of what I hoped for and certain of what I did not see. Owning a home of our own had become for Charles and me one of those impossible dreams people write and sing about. We had lived in an apartment for fourteen years. I was so sure we'd never own a house that I had even stopped praying about it.

Then in the fall of 1993, when real estate in southern California was in a slump, we found a condominium we loved—and could afford. It had a view of San Diego Bay from the living room, kitchen, dining room and master bedroom!

We pulled all our resources together: some retirement money, a small inheritance, passbook savings. Charles spent hours going over the figures before making an offer. I tingled at the thought of moving into our very own home. I was already planning a family picnic at the nearby park, a swimming party in the pool, and a Thanksgiving reunion in the recreation room of the complex.

The phone rang the next evening. "The owner has accepted your offer," our real estate agent said. "The place is yours."

I whooped with joy, then cried with gratitude: "Oh God, how gracious you are!" The next morning I began making plans for new carpet, fresh paint, maybe even a new dining room table.

Then Charles broke the news: There was no money for extras. "We'll be able to get in and cover closing costs," he said soberly. "It's going to be tight, but we can make it. We'll just have to do the carpet and paint as soon as we can."

"But I can't live with that horrible beige carpet," I whined. "And the walls! They're so . . . well, you know, used looking. I want everything fresh and clean when we move in."

"We have to wait," he said. "We don't have the money."

"You're right, we don't. But God does. I'm going to ask Him for it."

My words surprised my husband, but they surprised me even more. I had never taken such a bold step before, especially with God. But I knew in my heart that paint and carpet were part of the gift He had for us.

"It makes sense to make those changes before we move in," I said, trying to enlist my husband's support. "I feel certain the Lord will provide the money. I'm going to pray, believing."

Every morning I prayed in faith, "Lord, I thank you for the ten thousand dollars that is now hidden, and I trust you'll reveal it at the right time in the right place."

Several weeks later while Charles was having breakfast with his brother in Kentucky, some two thousand miles away from where we live, Charles shared with Robert what he called my "funny" prayer. Before he finished his story, a sly smile spread across Robert's face. "Charles, you're not going to believe this," he said, "but Mom has just released ten thousand dollars to each of us from Dad's estate. That was part of why I wanted to meet with you today."

Within weeks we had the money in hand. We called the painter, picked out carpet, scheduled the workers, banked the remaining funds, and moved in the same day the carpet layers completed the last room. Our God is an awesome God!

63

WORDS TO REFLECT ON

Praise be to the LORD, for he showed his wonderful love to me when I was in a besieged city. —PSALM 31:21

So then, just as you received Christ Jesus as Lord, continue to live in him, rooted and built up in him, strengthened in the faith as you were taught, and overflowing with thankfulness. —COLOSSIANS 2:6, 7

Now faith is being sure of what we hope for and certain of what we do not see. —HEBREWS 11:1

LOOKING WITHIN, LIVING IT OUT

- How have you responded to God's call to believe and give thanks for the things you cannot see?
- In what area of your life do you need to increase your faith and gratitude, despite the fact you can't see what God is up to?
- What is God asking you to believe Him for today?
- Write down something you're grateful for you do not yet see. Drop your slip into your Blessing Basket.

PRAYER STARTER

Dear God, thank you for the blessing of faith. I often overlook this gift because I am too focused on what I want, reserving my gratitude for when I receive it. But today I step out in faith, trusting you for what I cannot see—in my family, at work, in my personal life, in my community. Thank you that when I pray, believing, it is your pleasure to give me the kingdom.

Asking for Grace and Strength

 I BELIEVE THE Lord delights in our calls for help. But we often try to do things in our own strength first, turning to Him only after we've exhausted our efforts. I once heard a story about a man who continually misplaced his car keys. It became a source of humor and frustration in his household as his wife and children scurried around looking for Dad's lost keys.

One morning it was pouring rain and he was late for work. "Where are those blasted keys?" he shouted as he tore through the house searching drawers and closets and pockets.

His wife joined the search, but suddenly stopped, turned to her husband and said, "I'm tired of this routine. Why don't you ask the Holy Spirit where you put them?"

The man stopped, spun around and glared at her. "I'd rather do it myself first," he snapped.

How often we try to do for ourselves what only God can do—or what God can make easier for us to do if we simply ask Him for direction. But our pride gets in the way, and we fuss and fume as we attempt to work things out in our own power. We want to finish in the flesh what God has begun in the spirit. This is hardly good soil for cultivating a grateful heart. In fact, the more we do on our own, the less likely we are to turn our hearts to God in praise.

Ross Martinez, a Christian school principal, illustrated this point well. He had been concerned about a number of single-parent families he knew who were struggling. In an effort to encourage them to depend on God rather than on their own strength, he called a parent-teacher meeting to talk to them about his own experience.

"As most of you know, I'm a single dad," he said. "For years I tried to do things on my own strength. In fact, I took pride in being mother and father to my boys. I did everything. I cooked and kept up the house. We camped, and the kids played soccer and took music lessons. I enjoyed telling anyone who'd listen what a great dad I was!"

His face changed then as he took a deep breath and continued. "But it was a facade. My emotional life was a mess. The doctor said I had an ulcer. I had no time for myself, and I never made time for God. I stopped praying.

"And church? It was hit and miss—mostly miss. By Sunday I was always exhausted. I went on this way for several years until an elder from our church came over one evening and said, 'Let's talk. You look like you could use a friend.'

"I remember shrugging him off. 'Who me?' I asked. 'I'm fine.' He looked me square in the eye.

" 'No, you're not fine,' he said. 'When are you going to let God take over?' I can still remember my feelings as we sat there: pride, anger, resistance. I nearly choked on them. 'Brother,' he said softly, 'Let me pray for you. You need God. There is no more time or room in your life for pride. Let it go. Let God do what you cannot do. Do it for your kids, if not for yourself.'

"I had nothing to say. I broke down and cried. We prayed. I'm telling you this tonight because I know that some of you are trying to make it on your own strength. Stop! God wants to carry the weight for you. Let Him have your worry and fear and pride."

That parent-teacher meeting turned into a prayer meeting as parents came forward to acknowledge their needs before the Lord. According to Ross, "It was one of the most powerful and profound experiences I've had in all my years of education." What a great God we serve. He meets each one of us exactly where we are. How worthy of our praise and thanks He is.

67

WORDS TO REFLECT ON

Blessed is the man who makes the LORD his trust, who does not look to the proud, to those who turn aside to false gods. —PSALM 40:4

In all your ways acknowledge him, and he will make your paths straight. —PROVERBS 3:6

We have not received the spirit of the world but the Spirit who is from God, that we may understand what God has freely given us. —1 CORINTHIANS 2:12

LOOKING WITHIN, LIVING IT OUT

- In what areas of your life do you rely on your own strength?
- What steps can you take today to put them in God's hands?
- How can leaning on the Holy Spirit for guidance help you to develop a more grateful heart?
- Write down ways in which God has strengthened you. Thank Him and then place your paper into your Blessing Basket.

PRAYER STARTER

Father God, thank you that your grace is sufficient, that you are strong in my weakness, that it is your good pleasure to give me the kingdom when I seek you first. Help me today to seek you first in all my affairs, to turn to you before I turn to myself or to others. Remind me that you want to take care of me, to meet my needs, to give me the delight of my heart. I have your word on it. Thank you that your Word never returns void.

Praising God for What You Don't Have

WE CAN FILL UP our Blessing Baskets with praise for everything from good weather for the family picnic to recovery from a serious surgery. But have you ever thought about giving thanks for what you don't have—"thanks for nothing," as author Jessica Shaver phrases it?

"I'm grateful that for years now I haven't lost my contact lenses in rain-swollen gutters or in bowls of hot noodles. And I'm thankful that the phone call in the middle of the night was the wrong number and not someone calling to tell us about a death in the family."[1]

The list of things we don't have or that didn't happen might easily outnumber the list of things we do have and that did happen—if we stop and notice. Arnold, who wears Coke-bottle-thick glasses, says he's thankful he's not blind. Julie is grateful she didn't have a clothes dryer while living in Morocco because it forced her to hang her clothes outdoors, get acquainted with neighbors, and watch her children play in the courtyard, all at the same time.

Seventy-year-old Lou, a retired mail carrier, gives thanks for never owning a car. His job required he walk every day. "I stayed fit, kept my tan all year, saw neighbors and friends every day, and got paid to do it!"

Mrs. McNaughton, a 102-year-old resident in a nursing home, says she thanks God she's deaf. She can read her Bible and other books without the distraction of outside noises!

Maureen is grateful her kitchen didn't blow up when she left a pot of soup simmering on the stove while she went for a morning walk . . . and to the post office . . . and to the grocery store . . . before realizing what she had done!

Hector said he thanks God for all the colds he didn't catch, the car accidents he didn't get into because of driving too fast or too slow, and the debt he avoided by deciding not to buy a new car and computer.

I thank God for all the things He has not given me—like a huge estate on five acres of land. Too much cleaning and gardening! And too many servants to keep track of. I praise God I am short instead of tall. Store clerks can reach the high shelves for me, and my husband takes care of the cobwebs in the high corners.

I'm grateful my grandchildren don't live around the corner because I get to bring each one to my house for an individual visit. And when I go to their house I'm a special guest.

And I give thanks for not being a genius, a celebrity, a professional ice skater, a country-western singer, an engineer, a concert pianist or a famous surgeon. God knows what we need and don't need, and He always provides. We can thank Him for what we don't have as well as for what we do have.

WORDS TO REFLECT ON

The LORD will watch over your coming and going both now and forevermore. —PSALM 121:8

You will lie down, with no one to make you afraid, and many will court your favor. —JOB 11:19

Who is going to harm you if you are eager to do good? —1 PETER 3:13

LOOKING WITHIN, LIVING IT OUT

- Do you complain or do you praise God for the things He has not brought into your life?
- What can you thank God for not giving you?
- How can looking at what you don't have foster a more grateful heart?
- List at least five events or things that have not occurred in your life. Give thanks for them and then put your list into your Blessing Basket.

PRAYER STARTER

Dear God, I thank you for all that I have: a faithful spouse, a close friend, a job I love, a new computer, oatmeal cookies, a view of the bay, pine trees, Hallmark cards, good health, the Bible. And I thank you today as well for all that I don't have: terminal illness, unemployment, loud neighbors, a test to study for, lima beans on my dinner plate, standing in line for rations, living in a war zone . . . and so much more.

Note

1. Jessica Shaver, "Thanks for Nothing," *The Christian Communicator,* November 1996, 15.

Seeing the
Big Picture

 IF WE STAND too close to our daily lives we're likely to miss the big picture, so focused are we on the details—and often the inconsequential or negative ones at that. We miss the garden for the weeds. Such a stance hardly nurtures a grateful heart. Chances are, we feel resentful, not thankful.

When I am overwhelmed by the dailiness of my life I feel like grabbing my backpack and heading for the mountains. One morning I made arrangements to do just that! I woke in a snit. Everything seemed wrong. My writing wasn't going well. My husband and I couldn't agree on a decision we had to make. I'd had an upsetting phone call from a friend the night before. I knew a dose of mountain air and some hard exercise with my hiking buddies would clear my mind.

I called the leader and signed up for a trip the following weekend. Eight of us ventured out that bright morning committed to hike to the top of El Cajon Mountain in San Diego County. It was going to be a challenge. It was the highest peak in the area and there were no hiking trails at that time—just a fire road that zigzagged over the brushy terrain like a black ribbon turned loose.

After the first hour, we stopped for a water-and-shade break. One woman gazed at the five-hundred-foot descent in front of us and said with a trace of weariness in her voice, "I don't think I can take another dip. We gain and lose, gain and lose. What's the point? When are we going to get somewhere?"

One of the men looked out to the valley below. "Yes," he said, "but overall, we're going up." Pointing to the thick brush he added, "Soon as we get beyond this stuff, it'll be worth it."

That was enough for me; I was ready to move on. It sounded a lot like my life: I needed to get beyond the "stuff" that kept me tangled up and shortsighted. Later that morning, the same man shouted to those of us coming behind. "Hang in there! You're not going to believe this view. There's a great lookout point ahead."

He was right. The higher we climbed the more of the big picture we saw. Most important to me was our view from the top. Cars crawled along the freeway below. Houses looked like tiny wooden blocks—the kind we bargained for in Monopoly. Swimming pools were no more than bowls of water, and lawns appeared as specks of green sprinkled among concrete and asphalt. I had to laugh. The entire picture could be swallowed up in a flood, turned to ashes in a raging fire, or split open in a moment by an earthquake.

Yet I had focused on the details down there to such a degree that I had lost sight of the big picture. I knew in an instant why I was on that mountain that day: I needed to change my perspective. The higher we climb—whether up El Cajon Mountain or the mountain of life—the more of the big picture we see. We can't help but see it.

The abundant vistas overwhelm the details we create on the flatlands. The more we focus on God, the more of His plan we see and the more of His provision we receive. I came home that day realizing the best part of the trek was having the opportunity to view my life in a new way.

"Neither height nor depth, nor anything else in all creation, will be able to separate us from the love of God that is in Christ Jesus our Lord" (Romans 8:39)—if we make time to look at the big picture. My heart was full that night; full of gratitude.

WORDS TO REFLECT ON

Those who know your name will trust in you, for you, LORD, have never forsaken those who seek you. —PSALM 9:10

"Though the mountains be shaken and the hills be removed, yet my unfailing love for you will not be shaken nor my covenant of peace be removed," says the LORD, who has compassion on you. —ISAIAH 54:10

Get rid of all bitterness, rage and anger, brawling and slander, along with every form of malice. —EPHESIANS 4:31

LOOKING WITHIN, LIVING IT OUT

- How does focusing on details keep you from being grateful?
- In what areas can you trust in yourself less so you will trust and thank God more?
- What is your greatest challenge regarding being grateful?
- What is the most important gift God has given you? Write it down and drop the slip into your Blessing Basket.

PRAYER STARTER

Father God, thank you for the lookout points in my life, the rest stops that help me see the big picture instead of feeling consumed by the details that make up so much of my daily life. I praise you for your gentle reminders and patient guidance as you lead me up the mountain of life. I am grateful that today I have a new perspective.

Praising God for a New Point of View

SOMETIMES WE become so focused on living life from our viewpoint we nearly miss the joy that awaits us when we allow God to exchange our viewpoint for His. Peggy had such an experience during one of Billy Graham's crusades. She had heard it might be His last one so she determined to be in the audience that night at Ericcson Stadium.

She and her family and friends scouted for seats close to the stage, but there weren't any left by the time they arrived. The more they looked, the higher they climbed.

"The trek to the top was grueling," said Peggy. "Halfway up my legs became so weak, I wondered if I'd make it. When we finally got there I was upset to find myself sitting closer to the moon than to the stage on the playing field below."

That disappointment topped off a series of previous upsets. Peggy and her group had been in a traffic jam on the way to the stadium. So they arrived later than planned, with no time to eat dinner. There they were—rushed, grumpy, hungry and "sitting with our heads in the clouds," she joked.

"From our vantage point," she commented, "Billy Graham was just another dot among other indistinguishable dots far below!" Peggy said she was "brokenhearted," but she held back her thoughts. "Then," she added, "God tapped me on the shoulder. 'Peggy, I have some things to show you.'"

And what a show it was. Peggy said it began when the entire stadium of eighty thousand people stood to sing. "It was as though the heavens opened and a heavenly choir descended," she said. As people joined in song, hearts joined as well.

Even a flock of white birds participated by flying overhead in the gentle breeze. "But God had more to show me. To my amazement a very elderly man, dressed for church, including a hat and using a cane to brace himself, was climbing that mountain of steps with the aid of an attendant. Beads of perspiration poured down his face as I watched his final steps. He literally fell into the seat in front of me."

Peggy went on to say that God impressed on her the great determination of this man who was obviously in poor health. He was going to hear what the Lord had for him through Billy Graham, regardless of the cost.

"That night," confessed Peggy, "God took my eyes off myself and my circumstances and put them on more important things. I sang from the depth of my heart. I shed tears for the man who climbed the mountain. I rejoiced as the breeze caressed my face. And I was finally delighted to be sitting with my head in the clouds. I was that much closer to heaven!"

WORDS TO REFLECT ON

You, O LORD, keep my lamp burning; my God turns my darkness into light. —PSALM 18:28

For whoever exalts himself will be humbled, and whoever humbles himself will be exalted. —MATTHEW 23:12

Humble yourselves, therefore, under God's mighty hand, that he may lift you up in due time. —1 PETER 5:6

LOOKING WITHIN, LIVING IT OUT

79

- How have I refused God's gentle guidance and stubbornly clung to my own narrow point of view?
- In what ways does my perspective impede the cultivation of more gratitude?
- What can I do today to open myself more fully to God's point of view?
- Thank the Lord for the ways in which He has shared his vantage point with you. Write them down and drop the paper into your Blessing Basket.

PRAYER STARTER

Dear God, thank you for continuing to alter my point of view even when I resist, for showing me the gifts you have for me in the high places where I must climb to attain them, and in the low spots where I must stoop to claim them. Your ways are not my ways. Your vantage point is not mine. Remind me, teach me, show me and tutor me in the truth. Because you love me, you are willing to do that. You are awesome. I praise and thank you.

Forgiving Everything

 MANY PEOPLE have had a time in their life when the thought of forgiveness was so overwhelming they couldn't consider it. But because God knows how the root of bitterness can poison and strangle, He sometimes uses an unexpected episode to teach us how to forgive and then to give thanks.

This process can occur in an instant of realization or it can evolve over time. The last person I would have expected my lesson in forgiveness to come through was Lynn—the woman my husband left me for. The very name turned my stomach into a knot and caused my palms to dampen with anxiety.

But I couldn't escape it: Everywhere I went, I ran smack into that name. Lynn at the gym. Lynn on the tennis team. Lynn in my writing class. Rage and resentment were draining the life out of everything I did. I went to counseling. I read books. I talked to friends. I ran. I screamed into my pillow at night. I did everything I knew how to do—everything except forgive and let go.

Then one Saturday morning I attended a seminar on forgiveness at a neighborhood church. The leader asked us to close our eyes and bring to mind one person we needed to forgive. My first thought: Lynn, of course. My stomach churned. Yet something kept me in my seat. Lynn's image grew large in my mind. I opened my eyes. I lashed out at God. How can you expect me to forgive her? I shouted silently. But the Holy Spirit persisted. I can't, I insisted. She stole my husband. I didn't deserve what she did to me.

I felt so hot I could hardly breathe. Then just as quickly I felt cold enough to reach for my sweater. I wanted to release this woman who had plagued my every hour for months, but I also wanted to punish her with hateful thoughts. Hold on. Let go. Hold on. Let go.

Suddenly I couldn't bear the burden of my hatred any longer. The price was too great. Immediately, without warning, an incredible shift occurred. I can't describe it. I just—let go. For the first time in my life, I surrendered—and the Holy Spirit empowered me to do something I had stubbornly resisted. I released my grip on Lynn, on my ex-husband, on myself. I let go—just like that.

It was suddenly clear to me that as long as I separate myself from even one person, I separate myself from God. How self-righteous I had been. How arrogant!

The following Monday I wrote a letter to Lynn. I told her what had occurred, and I apologized for the hateful thoughts I had harbored against her.

On the following Wednesday, the phone rang. "Karen?" There was no mistaking her voice. "It's Lynn."

Surprisingly, my stomach remained calm, my hands dry, my voice steady. I listened more than I talked—unusual for me. I found myself actually interested in what she had to say. She thanked me for the letter, and then told me how sorry she was for everything. All I had wanted to hear from her, I heard that day.

As I replaced the receiver, however, I noticed that none of it mattered. I appreciated her response, but it was suddenly unimportant. I had finally discovered what I'd been looking for: the assurance that God was with me, encouraging and strengthening me. No one can take my good away. My life is a gift from God and every experience, no matter how painful or confusing or hurtful, can draw me closer to Him if I allow it to. He has taught me how to forgive—and then to give thanks—in everything.

WORDS TO REFLECT ON

Wait for the LORD; be strong and take heart and wait for the LORD. —PSALM 27:14

Do not say, "I'll pay you back for this wrong!" Wait for the LORD, and he will deliver you. —PROVERBS 20:22

And when you stand praying, if you hold anything against anyone, forgive him, so that your Father in heaven may forgive you your sins. —MARK 11:25

83

LOOKING WITHIN,
LIVING IT OUT

- Who are you holding hostage for the hurts they've inflicted on you?

- Are you willing to forgive them? What must you do to begin to make this a reality?
- How does forgiveness, or lack of it, impact your experience and expression of gratitude?
- Write down at least one thing you're grateful for as a result of extending or receiving forgiveness and add it to your Blessing Basket.

PRAYER STARTER

Lord Jesus, you loved me enough to lay down your life for me, a sinner. I thank you today that through your example and grace I am able to forgive my enemies and to ask forgiveness of those I have sinned against. I no longer want to live in a state of bitterness. I want to embrace gratitude, resting in the assurance that you are my God, the dispenser of all justice.

Sharing God's Love

 WITHOUT LOVE, as Paul reminds us in 1 Corinthians 13:1, we become a "sounding gong or a clanging cymbal." Nothing else matters if we don't have love. Even gratitude is a clanging cymbal if love is not its driving force.

Love is much more than a feeling that comes and goes like a morning breeze. Love is a decision. Love requires discipline. We know from our own experience the healing power of God's love. Without His love we wouldn't be able to put the past to rest, start fresh in the present, and hope for what is yet to come. No lasting transformation can occur in our lives without God's love.

The decision to love also challenges us to express love according to God's will, not our whims. And when we love with His guidance and counsel, He will give us the means to remain faithful as spouses, parents and friends. He will free us to see and experience the love others have for us. Nowhere is the giving and receiving of love more evident than in our closest relationships.

Those who truly love us stand by us. They teach us that love is patient. They don't blow up if we're late for a dinner date or if we have to work overtime once in a while. And they continue to love us even when we disagree or disappoint them. They show by example that love is kind. They remember we're human, still learning and growing, and that we make mistakes sometimes. And they seem to know that criticizing us doesn't help us change for the better. They teach us that love is not jealous. They give us room to develop at our own pace. They don't object if we want to take a class or take a nap!

We sense they respect us and trust our decisions. We learn by their example that love does not take into account a wrong suffered. They don't blame or burden us with their hurts. They don't wear their pain like a badge of honor or get stuck in criticism and complaint. They show by their own lives that it's healthier to live in the present than to linger in the past.

These special people show us that love never fails. They don't withhold their love until we shape up, measure up or live up to their standards. We've learned through them that love is faithful and honest and loyal, no matter what.

Because they love us, we can choose to be patient when they are late, make a mistake, are in a bad mood or misunderstand. We can give back to them by surprising them with little gifts, taking them out to lunch or to the beach, listening when they're feeling down, praying with them when they need a touch of grace. When they spend time alone or with their friends or talk excitedly about a project or event that doesn't include us, we can be happy for them, not jealous.

We know there's room for more than one love in their lives. Because of what they've taught us, we can give up taking into account a wrong suffered. We can be slower to judge and quicker to forgive. We can choose to stand by them, believe in them and expect the best from them. Those who love us teach us that love is what really matters. Everything else will pass away. Messy rooms, forgotten appointments, dirty laundry, cold meals and hurt feelings—they are all temporary. Only love lasts forever.

WORDS TO REFLECT ON

"Because he loves me," says the LORD, "I will rescue him; I will protect him, for he acknowledges my name."
PSALM 91:14

I will heal their waywardness and love them freely, for my anger has turned away from them. —HOSEA 14:4

Dear friends, let us love one another, for love comes from God. Everyone who loves has been born of God and knows God. Whoever does not love does not know God, because God is love . . . Dear friends, since God so loved us, we also ought to love one another. —JOHN 4:7, 8, 11

LOOKING WITHIN, LIVING IT OUT

- How has being loved affected your expression of gratitude?
- What specifically can you do today to show your love for God and others?
- How have you experienced love as a gift?
- Write out a list of ways you give and receive love and then add the list to your Blessing Basket.

PRAYER STARTER

Dear God, I thank you for the gift of love. I wouldn't even know what it means if you hadn't first loved me. But you did . . . and you still do. I praise you for all the ways you demonstrate your love for me each day. My list of things to be grateful for is growing. But at the top of my list is your love, manifested through your Son, Jesus, and through the loving people in my life. I thank you for all of them.

Keeping Promises

 IT'S EASIER TO point our finger at someone than to turn it toward ourselves. We all have ideas of how other people should change, but when it comes to our own growth many of us find refuge in bumper-sticker theology: "Be patient. God's not finished with me yet!"

Jesus revealed His penetrating understanding of our hearts when He asked the challenging question, "How can you say to your brother, 'Let me take the speck out of your eye,' when all the time there is a plank in your own eye?" (Matthew 7:4).

This verse hit home for me one evening as my husband lay sprawled on the sofa, tie loosened, feet propped on the coffee table. The television hummed in the background. The newspaper lay in a pile on the floor. A bowl of half-finished popcorn was perched on his abdomen, rising and falling with each breath he took. It was a familiar sight, one I had grown accustomed to over the years. I wanted to shake Charles awake and tear into him with my frustration, my anger, my loneliness.

Our wonderful periods of togetherness and intimacy were too often followed by these sudden unexplained voids of work, sleep, food, television. They frightened me. He always did the laundry. He fixed things around the house. He told me every day he loved me. Yet I knew his heart was heavy.

He was scared, lonely, angry. He desperately wanted to use his life for a good purpose—speaking, writing, teaching—but he felt stuck in a job that paid little and didn't feel right. He didn't know how to make it different.

And I couldn't make it different for him. I, too, was scared and lonely and angry. But it wouldn't do any good to confront Charles. I had already tried. I couldn't change him. I didn't even know how to change myself. Only God could snatch Charles from the abyss he had been hovering over. And only God could transform the way I responded to him.

God did both. Unexpectedly, wonderfully, along came Promise Keepers, a movement for Christian men that motivates and inspires them to make seven life-changing promises. Keeping these promises can transform men's relationships with God, their families, their churches and their communities. When meetings sprung up at our church, they caught my husband's attention. He attended a convention in Los Angeles. His convictions changed.

Then our pastor approached Charles and some other men, inviting them to be mentors to younger men in our congregation by starting Man Alive home groups. Charles jumped at the opportunity. "It's what I've always wanted to do," he told me. "We can learn together and grow and help each other keep our promises."

Monday night after Monday night, men came to our home. The sounds of their talking and sharing and praying together

filled our house. They were learning to build more vital relationships with God, friends, family and church. They were coming
to terms with what it means to live with integrity, to be committed to one another and to a world desperately in need of the person and power of Jesus Christ. And so was I.

As God changed my husband, He changed me as well. The
Lord assured me in prayer that Charles was doing fine. He was,
after all, in good hands! So I put my attention on the Lord—
where it belonged. I put prayer at the top of my list. And I saw
my husband do the same thing.

After several weeks, our private prayer led to corporate
prayer. Praying together each morning opened the way to more
intimacy. We started talking again—and listening. He shared his
struggles and asked for my support. I agreed. Then I shared mine
and asked him to stand by me. He agreed. Day by day, week after
week, one month after another we continued to pray first, talk
and listen, then do things together, from the commonplace—such
as grocery shopping—to the creative—such as organizing a family picnic or attending a concert.

We are continuing to rebuild our marriage. Sometimes we
retreat to old ways—too much television and popcorn and too
much reminding and cajoling—but we catch ourselves now, and
we're able to stop before we lose our way. Keeping our promises
to one another is not nearly the challenge it once was because
now we are in fellowship each day with the greatest Promise
Keeper of all.

WORDS TO REFLECT ON

He remembers his covenant forever, the word he commanded, for a thousand generations. —PSALM 105:8

For the LORD your God is a merciful God; he will not abandon or destroy you or forget the covenant with your forefathers, which he confirmed to them by oath. —DEUTERONOMY 4:31

I pray that you may be active in sharing your faith, so that you will have a full understanding of every good thing we have in Christ. —PHILEMON 6

LOOKING WITHIN, LIVING IT OUT

- How have other people's broken promises kept you from being grateful?
- What can you do to make amends for your own broken promises?
- How does making or breaking your promises impact your desire to praise and thank God?
- Jot down the promises of God you are most thankful for and add them to your Blessing Basket.

PRAYER STARTER

Dear Jesus, you are the consummate Promise Keeper. "The Lord is not slow in keeping his promise, as some understand slowness. He is patient with you, not wanting anyone to perish, but everyone to come to repentance" (2 Peter 3:9). You have brought me to repentance and to gratitude for growth and change in myself and in those I love. Oh God, what would have become of me if you had not kept your promises? My heart overflows with thanksgiving.

93

Giving Thanks for Children

"**I TELL YOU** the truth, unless you change and become like little children, you will never enter the kingdom of heaven" (Matthew 18:3). What powerful words. Entrance into the kingdom of heaven does not require a college degree or advanced age or dignified behavior. Jesus says, simply, "Become like little children."

Who could be in the company of children for long without experiencing the wisdom of Jesus' words and the call He has put on our lives to become like them? Children speak truth: "I hate those green things, Mom, but I sure like the noodles."

They exude innocence: "Daddy, can I call Grandpa in heaven?" They exhibit spontaneity: "Try to catch me, Grandma. I bet you can't!" They model unconditional faith: "I know God loves me. He tells me every day."

They open our hearts and sometimes stop us in our tracks with their love and affection and trust: "Daddy, can I marry you when I grow up?" "Grammy, I wish you lived next door so my daddy and I could find you every day." "Mommy, I like it when you tickle my back. It feels like angel wings."

Children also wear us down and sometimes wear us thin! "I must have answered sixteen 'why' questions without a break," says the mother of a toddler.

"If I could have twenty minutes to myself, I think I could make it till dinner," adds another.

Sometimes it's a challenge to be with kids, and it's awful without them. Once they're part of our lives, we will never be the same. We learn, in a whole way, what being thankful really means.

Pat's story is a good illustration of the joyful tension we live in and the gratitude we feel as children teach us what it takes to enter the kingdom of heaven.

"As the jet carried my two children off to Grandma's house in Ohio, I began to like the idea of what lay ahead," Pat says. "No spilled milk. No footprints on the yellow carpet. No slamming doors for two whole weeks!" Pat and her husband planned to rediscover each other. They looked forward to adult conversation at dinner, walking on the beach, and leisurely Saturdays that began at 10:30 a.m. instead of 6:30 a.m.

"I was anticipating having time to think and talk and shower and pray without interruption," Pat says, "and to cook spinach lasagna without criticism. And Ted and I could play golf at eight in the morning or five in the afternoon."

Pat's fantasy took shape so quickly she could barely keep up with it. The vacation from parenthood began Sunday afternoon. The first night Pat and Ted enjoyed dinner and a movie with friends. On Monday Pat cleaned her home office and tackled some neglected files. On Tuesday she read a book and met a friend for a walk and lunch. Wednesday she joined her husband for a baseball game. Thursday she started on a new writing assignment. And Friday she waxed the kitchen floor and did laundry.

"The second week," she says with tears in her eyes, "I found myself wandering into my children's Lysol-clean rooms and actually longing for the sight of scattered socks and open drawers. I missed the sound of little fingers at the piano and my son's basketball against the backboard."

Pat liked not tripping over her son's skateboard for a week, but she didn't like not getting good-night hugs and kisses. "I remember turning to my husband one night and saying, 'It's not going the way I thought it would. Molly and Tommy are part of our lives now. It will never be just the two of us again.' And I knew then I didn't want it to be."

Pat says time away from her children permanently changed her attitude. "I thank God for those kids every day now. What a gift they are!"

WORDS TO REFLECT ON

Your wife will be like a fruitful vine within your house; your sons will be like olive shoots around your table. —PSALM 128:3

All your sons will be taught by the LORD, and great will be your children's peace. —ISAIAH 54:13

Therefore, whoever humbles himself like this child is the greatest in the kingdom of heaven. —MATTHEW 18:4

LOOKING WITHIN, LIVING IT OUT

- Who are the children in your life? What can you learn from them?
- In what ways do you need to become more childlike?
- Why does the Lord want you to become like a child in order to enter the kingdom of heaven?
- Write down the names of the children you are grateful for. Reflect on their gifts to you. Then drop your paper into your Blessing Basket.

PRAYER STARTER

Lord God, how I thank you for the children in my life, for the example they are to me. I want to be more like them: truthful, playful, spontaneous, grateful. You have given me so much; give me one thing more: the heart of a child so I might enter the kingdom of heaven and thank you for all eternity.

Transforming Your Mind

OUR MINDS ARE transformed when we apply our thoughts to things that cause transformation. Paul encourages us in Philippians 4:8 to think about and meditate on things that are true and pure and noble. What could be more worthy of our meditation than praise and thanksgiving? And yet I came to this understanding the hard way.

Some years ago, with little warning, my husband lost his job. Within a few months, my freelance writing opportunities dwindled as well. We prayed and asked others to pray for us. We drew on our savings account. We cashed in investments. We sold some property. Before long, we were using our last reserves. I panicked. Why this, Lord? I prayed. We're willing to work. Please show us what to do!

God answered, but not in the way I'd imagined. One Sunday an envelope with Charles's name on it arrived at the church office.

It contained an anonymous note with an encouraging passage of Scripture and enough cash to tide us over for a couple of weeks. About the time that ran out, people in our fellowship group sent us checks. The more our friends reached out to us, the more upset I became. I said "thank you" but I didn't feel grateful; I felt resentful.

This wasn't the way it was supposed to be. On one hand, we needed their support, but on the other, I felt uneasy as my sense of indebtedness and obligation mounted. Some part-time teaching helped keep us going a while longer, but our bills were greater than my income, so we began to slip again.

One month, when our rent was due and our checking account was empty, Charles asked for help from the deacon's fund at our church. To me that was the final blow. The deacon's fund was for the poor—people in real need. That profile didn't fit us; we had always given to the fund, not taken from it.

Though I felt gratitude when the check arrived, I was ashamed because we needed it so badly. Slowly I realized how unaccustomed I was to receiving. It simply wasn't part of my lifestyle. Receiving made me feel vulnerable to others and to God. I didn't like the feeling.

The following month a surprise check from my parents arrived. They did not even know about our financial trouble. On my husband's birthday, more money came in. As each gift arrived I forced myself to stop and give thanks. My heart began to change. Who was I to decide how God chose to provide for us? If I truly believed God is my source, then I needed to step aside and watch Him do what only He can do.

Shortly before Christmas that year we received a money order for the exact amount we needed for our tree, holiday food and a few gifts. It was signed "Barnabas"—a fitting pseudonym. Charles and I looked at each other in disbelief.

Then the tears came. "Thank God!" we shouted. For an entire year, He had kept us going despite our clumsy attempts to interrupt the process. By mid-January, things began to turn around almost as suddenly as they had fallen apart. My freelance work picked up, and Charles received several promising job leads. It seemed the Lord had finally broken through to us.

Our minds had been transformed, our attitude made new and our hearts softened as God met our every need. It had been our season to receive, our turn to be humbled before God and our friends, and our time to learn the meaning of giving thanks.

WORDS TO REFLECT ON

From the LORD comes deliverance. —PSALM 3:8

They will not toil in vain or bear children doomed to misfortune; for they will be a people blessed by the LORD, they and their descendants with them. Before they call I will answer; while they are still speaking I will hear. —ISAIAH 65:23, 24

So do not worry, saying, "What shall we eat?" or "What shall we drink?" or "What shall we wear?" For the pagans run after all these things, and your heavenly Father knows that you need them. —MATTHEW 6:31, 32

LOOKING WITHIN, LIVING IT OUT

- Have you allowed others to give to you, or do you prefer to give?
- Can you share your needs and weaknesses, or must you always be in control?
- How can being vulnerable with others help you develop a more grateful heart?
- Write down two ways in which the Lord has provided for you even when you resisted. Thank Him for them, then add them to your Blessing Basket.

PRAYER STARTER

Dear God, thank you for your faithfulness to me, for providing my every need from the moment I was conceived in my mother's womb. There has not been a day in my life when you have taken your eye off me. You promised to lead me on the path I should take, to carry my load, to comfort me in sorrow, to give me bread for each day. I praise your name and give you thanks for all you have done for me.

Living in
Kingdom Time

WHEN YOU turn to a new week in your calendar, are you struck by the many things left undone from the previous week or month—letters you planned to write, clothes you hoped to sort and give away, house repairs you forgot to schedule, flowers that need tending, cluttered cabinets crying for an ordering hand?

Time! If only there was more of it. Or more energy to accomplish our goals in the time we have. But wait! Do we want to keep falling prey to the tyranny of time management?

Time management tools—date books, pocket calendars, wrist watches with built-in alarms, beepers for belt or handbag, best-selling books, computer programs and seminars on how to save, spend, invest and maximize time before it flies away—inundate our culture.

What if time was not the fleeting, tyrannizing resource we've learned to believe it is? What if we chose instead to view time as an expression of God? God's speed. God's gift to us. A part of His very nature. Would we so anxiously live by deadlines, join the morning rat race or grab a minute and run with it? Would we, instead, rethink and perhaps reshape the way we use time? Perhaps our goal would be stewardship rather than management.

As stewards we might be more open to the purposes set down by the Chief Steward. Rather than accomplishing and accumulating according to some self-imposed deadline, we might share our time by serving others in Jesus' name. We might choose to spend a serendipity Saturday with one of our children or grandchildren—not counting the hours, but enjoying the time together.

We might drop by a community convalescent home and make a few bedside calls—not worrying that we can't see everyone, but thanking God for the one loving word, one warm touch, or one prayer whispered with whomever the Lord puts in our path.

103

We might devote an afternoon to prayer or Scripture reading—not feeling guilty for having neglected the closets or the garden, just content with having exchanged the daily race for a period of grace. Time spent in these ways has eternal value. Rather than accounting for something, we make ourselves accountable to the One in charge. We replace the insane race against the clock with a peaceful surrender to the desires and direction of the Giver. The interesting and arresting result of this way of living is a miraculous expansion of time—periods of grace that allow us to give and take, to serve and to receive, to work and to rest without feeling busy or lazy. When Jesus announced His ministry He proclaimed, "The time has come . . . The kingdom of God is near" (Mark 1:15).

When we walk with Jesus we join His mission in the world as we weave the threads of our allotted time into a tapestry of eternal significance. Those of us who have heeded His call do not have to wait for heaven to experience the peace Christ promises to those who follow Him.

Kingdom grace is available now if we're willing to live in kingdom time. Let's respond to the call. Let's take the time and receive the grace to set our clocks and our calendars according to God's agenda and to reorder our lives around His values, His commandments and His priorities. Let's learn His "timeless" management.

WORDS TO REFLECT ON

If the LORD delights in a man's way, he makes his steps firm. —PSALM 37:23

Keep your lives free from the love of money and be content with what you have, because God has said, "Never will I leave you; never will I forsake you." —HEBREWS 13:5

But godliness with contentment is great gain. —1 TIMOTHY 6:6

LOOKING WITHIN, LIVING IT OUT

- How have you allowed the tyranny of time to keep you from being grateful?
- In what ways have you let yourself be controlled by your clock and calendar instead of by God?
- What are you most grateful for about kingdom time?
- How has God's "timeless management" blessed you? Write it down and put it into your Blessing Basket.

PRAYER STARTER

Faithful God, thank you that you are timeless and that your love for me is without constraints of any kind. I praise you that when I seek you first, everything else falls into place. There is no tyranny in kingdom time for you are not a hostage to the clock or the calendar. When I pray, you give me your undivided attention. My heart is full of gratitude today for the gift of kingdom time.

Dwelling in Joy

 HOW CAN WE thank God enough for you in return for all the joy we have in the presence of our God because of you?" (1 Thessalonians 3:9). When we are faithful to God, through practice and trust, we cannot help but exude joy. This is what Paul saw in the Thessalonians. And the joy he witnessed inspired him to gratitude.

Joy entwines with gratitude. As we praise and thank God, we experience joy, and as we express joy, our hearts again turn to gratitude. Jesus is our model for a joy-filled life. Joy marked His entry into the world when the angel announced, "Do not be afraid. I bring you good news of great joy that will be for all the people" (Luke 2:10). Then as He prepared to leave the earth, Jesus encouraged His followers to live in His fullness: "I have told you this so that my joy may be in you and that your joy may be complete" (John 15:11).

Paul listed joy as one of the fruit of the Spirit (Galatians 5:22), and he reminded the Galatians to bear witness of the Spirit in their lives: "Since we live by the Spirit, let us keep in step with the Spirit" (Galatians 5:25).

I believe that same reminder applies to us today. We too must keep in step with the Spirit by echoing the words of the psalmist: "My mouth shall praise you with joyful lips" (Psalm 63:5). Regardless of what is going on in our lives, we can respond with a heart full of joy because we know:

- our Redeemer lives,
- that all things work together for good to those who love God,
- and that our Lord will never leave us nor forsake us.

Joy is the natural response to such jubilant promises!

Richard Foster writes, "If we fill our lives with simple good things and constantly thank God for them, we will know joy."[1]

Fill your life today with "simple good things"—a beautiful sunset, homemade soup, a loved one's voice on the phone, children playing and laughing, a cup of mint tea, a long walk with a good friend, time to read, time to pray. Gratitude leads to joy and joy to gratitude. It's contagious! Spread it around—like apple butter on hot muffins. You will create such a fragrant aroma that everyone you come into contact with will want to get closer. What an opportunity this is to share the true source of your joy and gratitude—Jesus Christ—and to invite others into a relationship of their own with Him. "Enter his gates with thanksgiving and his courts with praise; give thanks to him and praise his name" (Psalm 100:4).

WORDS TO REFLECT ON

You have made known to me the path of life; you will fill me with joy in your presence, with eternal pleasures at your right hand. —PSALM 16:11

I will rejoice in the LORD, I will be joyful in God my Savior. —HABAKKUK 3:18

Now is your time of grief, but I will see you again and you will rejoice, and no one will take away your joy. —JOHN 16:22

LOOKING WITHIN, LIVING IT OUT

- What areas of your life are cause for joy?
- In what ways have you allowed fear and worry to sabotage your expression of joy and gratitude?
- How does a joyful attitude correlate with a grateful heart?
- Consider the things you are most joyful about. Thank God for these gifts. Write them down and put them into your Blessing Basket.

PRAYER STARTER

Dear God, thank you that gratitude begets joy and joy begets gratitude. What a lovely cycle to dwell in. I praise you today for the many simple good things in my life and for the joy they bring to me. Let me continue to challenge myself, to release my fear, to abandon my worry about what others think, and simply let my mouth praise you with joyful lips so that every word is a hymn of thanksgiving.

Note

1. Richard Foster, *Celebration of Discipline* (San Francisco: Harper & Row, 1978), 167.

Giving Thanks for Having Enough

LIVING IN A land of plenty presents a challenge. A climate of aggressive advertising and conspicuous consumption often distorts our vision of what is enough. Advertisers tell us our wants—a new outfit, a nice car, a theater ticket, a vacation—are really our needs. Even though I see the fallacy of this thinking, I still succumb. When I focus my attention on what I think I need, I'm less inclined to give thanks for what I have and to be grateful that what I have is enough.

This truth came home to me in an unexpected and dramatic way while on a trip to Mexico. After arriving in Los Mochis, we spent our first full day in the village of Cerocahui. That evening following dinner and mariachi music, my husband and I said good night to our friends and walked back to our room. The moment I opened the door I knew something was wrong. Someone had pushed aside the curtain on the window facing the street, and the window was wide open. It had not been that way when we left or when my husband had returned less than an hour before to pick up our sweaters.

Then it hit me. Someone robbed us! Our duffel bags and packs stowed on the floor beside the dresser were gone. I checked under the beds, around the floor, in the closet, in the bathroom. Nothing. Some person had cleaned us out. Our camera was missing as well. All that remained were some snacks, our pajamas, and a few papers and maps. My heart raced. I was nearly sick.

I ran out of the room and into the office. "*Señor*," I shouted, "there's been a theft in room 104. Our bags, our packs are gone."

Within the hour, the manager and the police chief were at our door to take a report and to reassure us they would do everything they could to retrieve our belongings. All we could do was wait—and pray. It was only the second day of our nine-day trip. I couldn't imagine wearing the same outfit for seven more days!

Then the sad thought of not being able to take pictures came over me. Next I remembered that my books were in one of my bags. No reading for a week! And then the horrible realization came that even my wallet, with credit cards, driver's license, passport, health insurance card and seventy dollars in cash, had been nestled inside my stolen pack in preparation for the next day's hike.

"Lord, what now?" I cried. "I need these things. How will we get along the rest of the week?"

Within seconds a gentle peace came over me, and I recalled the familiar scripture where Jesus reminds His followers not to worry about clothes and food. If God cares for the flowers and the birds, how much more will He care for me. (Matthew 6:25–30)

I knew then I did have enough—for that moment—which is all that mattered. Pajamas to sleep in, toiletries and toothbrush, my husband by my side, shoes and clothes for the next day, and snacks for the bus ride.

"And you have me," God seemed to say. "I will not leave you nor forsake you."

With that assurance I drifted off to sleep. The next morning we recovered a few items down by the stream as we crossed over to hike up to a waterfall. A pair of socks discarded here, a shirt thrown there, a couple of pairs of my husband's pants, still folded, lying on the bank. Later that afternoon fellow travelers offered to loan us hats and shirts and money. When we arrived at the next hotel on our itinerary, we discovered the hotel manager where the robbery had taken place had wired ahead to request complimentary meals and beverages during our stay.

As we checked in, the desk clerk loaned us his camera with a new roll of film already loaded! The next day we relaxed. We weren't going to let this incident ruin the trip for us or for others. We put it behind us and joined the group for a hike in the mountains. That afternoon the hotel manager approached me in the lobby.

"Some more of your things will arrive by bus this afternoon at three," she said. To our surprise, at that very hour, the bus driver walked in with a large black trash bag bundled tight. Inside? Our two duffels and daypacks bulging with belongings the police had recovered.

My husband got back everything except one glove! And I received about 90 percent of my belongings. My cards and papers and money were not among them, nor was the camera, but I knew I could replace those when I got home. As for the cash, well, the complimentary meals and beverages more than made up for that loss.

We couldn't stop thanking our wonderful Lord and we didn't care who heard us. The bags were full—but not as full as our hearts. We had enough, indeed—more than enough with Christ at our side.

WORDS TO REFLECT ON

I will praise God's name in song and glorify him with thanksgiving. —PSALM 69:30

With praise and thanksgiving they sang to the LORD: "He is good; his love to Israel endures forever." And all the people gave a great shout of praise to the LORD, because the foundation of the house of the LORD was laid. —EZRA 3:11

For everything God created is good, and nothing is to be rejected if it is received with thanksgiving. —1 TIMOTHY 4:4

113

LOOKING WITHIN, LIVING IT OUT

- How have you confused your needs and wants?
- How has this confusion impacted your inclination to give thanks in all things?
- What have you learned from today's reading about what is enough?
- What needs has God filled for you? Write them down and then drop your slip of paper into your Blessing Basket.

PRAYER STARTER

Oh Lord, how faithful you are to me. Even when I forget your promises, you remain constant in my life, protecting me and providing for me. When I think of the trees and flowers of the field and the birds of the air, I am humbled by how you care for them. They simply are! They don't do anything. They remain in the place where you have planted them and they reflect your glory. I want to be like that, dear God—one whose very being is an expression of gratitude and praise.

Finding Blessings in Unlikely Places

 "KNOWING GOD is the most astounding thing that has ever happened to me," says Carmen. "After years of struggling with the fear of lack (I always thought I'd end up a bag lady), I feel God is telling me there is plenty for me.

"I've always had a hard time buying the clothes I need. I didn't think I deserved anything nice. I shopped garage sales and thrift shops. I remember once, years ago, wanting a new suit for work, but I couldn't bring myself to buy one. Spending money on myself seemed wrong somehow. I wore an old T-shirt to bed for years, even though I dreamed of sleeping in a white silk nightgown.

"Then the most astounding thing happened. One day as my husband and I were driving home, I noticed something white and shimmering lying in the street. I had to stop. My husband pulled over, and when I jumped out of the car I saw a beautiful white nightgown—embossed, stylish and brand new! In fact, it still had the store tag on it."

Carmen picked up the nightgown, hopped back in the car and thanked God. "I told Him that however He chooses to bring things into my life is great with me."

Another time Carmen needed a pair of size-six low-heeled red pumps to go with a suit for a wedding, but she didn't have the money. God delivered again.

Her grandmother, who wore the same size shoes, gave her the exact pair she had wanted, without even knowing Carmen was in need.

"I'm such a practical person," she says. "At times I've struggled with my faith in God." But Carmen now admits God is removing her doubts in some pretty practical and unexpected ways. And she is learning to give thanks in all things.

116

WORDS TO REFLECT ON

I will not violate my covenant or alter what my lips have uttered. —PSALM 89:34

O LORD, you are my God; I will exalt you and praise your name, for in perfect faithfulness you have done marvelous things, things planned long ago. —ISAIAH 25:1

Let us hold unswervingly to the hope we profess, for he who promised is faithful. —HEBREWS 10:23

LOOKING WITHIN, LIVING IT OUT

- How has God blessed you in an unexpected way? What was your response?
- How have God's surprises helped you turn your heart toward gratitude?
- How have God's blessings impacted the way you treat others?
- Jot down two or more of God's unexpected blessings. Thank Him for them and drop the paper into your Blessing Basket.

PRAYER STARTER

Lord God, I thank you for the way you bless me in unexpected ways. I think I have things all figured out and then—surprise! You turn things upside down and show me who's really in charge. And I'm so glad you are. I know you have my best interests in mind even when I don't. You provide for me regardless of my distorted beliefs and thoughts. I praise you and thank you for your awesome and tangible presence in my life.

117

Offering the Sacrifice of Praise

 "HE WHO OFFERS a sacrifice of thanksgiving honors Me" (Psalm 50:23). Just think! By lifting up prayers of praise and gratitude, we honor God. What could be more pleasurable, more worthy of our time, more encouraging to our spirits? All we need to do is keep our eyes open, our hearts in tune with God, our lips ready to praise. The blessings are there. It is up to us to open our mouths and give thanks.

Remember the story of the woman at the well in the fourth chapter of John's Gospel? She came intending to fill a jar with water. She went home with the entire supply! Imagine the gratitude that filled her mouth as she walked home that day.

And how about the centurion who, after the death of Jesus on the cross, proclaimed, "Surely this was a righteous man" (Luke 23:47). In that moment he honored God with his praise. Jesus Himself honored the Father with His thanksgiving.

"Taking the five loaves and the two fish and looking up to heaven, he gave thanks and broke the loaves. Then he gave them to his disciples to set before the people" (Mark 6:41). And there was plenty for everyone.

Consider ways to honor God each day with your prayers of praise. Ask someone to join you. Take turns lifting your hearts and words to God, praising Him for His protection, provision and power.

Name the things that come to mind: the illness you survived, the money you needed for a particular purchase, the friend who came along and helped with your work load, the child who taught you how to laugh again, the answer that came to you when you least expected it, the opportunity that turned up when you had nearly given up hope.

Like David the psalmist, you may wish to honor God in song. One woman told me she likes to dance through her house when she is alone, singing her gratitude to God. Or you may prefer to simply dialogue with God.

"I talk to Christ all day," says one man I know. "I thank Him for anything and everything you can imagine!"

Acknowledge God for who He is: your Abba Father. Spend time worshiping Him in song, thanking Him in conversation, praising Him in written prayer, resting in Him through quiet contemplation.

119

WORDS TO REFLECT ON

Evening, morning and noon I cry out in distress, and he hears my voice. —PSALM 55:17

The LORD is far from the wicked but he hears the prayer of the righteous. —PROVERBS 15:29

They will be my people, and I will be their God. —JEREMIAH 32:38

LOOKING WITHIN, LIVING IT OUT

- What does prayer mean to you?
- How are prayer and gratitude related in your life?
- Are your prayers focused on petition or praise? What should be the purpose of your prayers?
- Thank God for answered prayer. Write down some of the ways God has responded to your prayers and drop that paper into your Blessing Basket.

120

PRAYER STARTER

Lord God, thank you for the lifeline of prayer. What a gift! You not only speak to me, you want me to speak my heart to you. You have said that every time I offer a sacrifice of thanksgiving I honor you. What a blessing to know that. It is easy to thank you, God. Everything I am and have I owe to you. How could I not praise you? For you are my God, and I am your grateful child.

Accepting Opportunities

 ONE DAY AS Paul, Barnabas, Symeon and Manaen—all part of the church at Antioch—were fasting and praying, the Holy Spirit said, "Dedicate Barnabas and Paul for a special job I have for them" (Acts 13:2). So the others laid hands on the two and sent them on their way.

This passage offers some spectacular insights into how God lets us know what He wants of us and for us. To me, the most striking insight is this: The Holy Spirit directs God's work among His people. That truth alone should be enough to get our attention. We can trust when God calls, He also guides.

I experienced this a few months ago following the death of one of our good friends. Cliff died unexpectedly from heart failure, leaving his wife and two young children as well as two teenagers from his previous marriage. I couldn't get my mind off little Sarah, eight, and Brian, six. Their daddy was gone. In addition, their maternal grandmother had died just two months before, and their paternal grandparents had died days apart two years prior to that. Their maternal grandfather had Alzheimer's so he couldn't be present in their lives, and their one uncle lived in Alaska—thousands of miles away.

These children had experienced so much loss so early in their lives, I could hardly take it in. The Sunday following Cliff's death we invited his wife, Glenda, and the two children to brunch so we could talk and reminisce and comfort one another.

While seated at the restaurant, Sarah seemed listless and disinterested in talking or eating. Brian picked at his food and clung to his mother as we talked. Suddenly a thought came to me. I leaned over to Sarah and asked her if I could rub her back.

"When we're sad," I said, "sometimes it helps to have someone who loves us touch us or hold us close." She moved a little but didn't say anything, so I gently massaged her back and played with her hair.

Within moments, she sat up and snuggled her full weight into my side. My eyes filled with tears. "Since you don't have a living grandma," I said, "I'm wondering if you'd like to adopt me! I have gray hair and wrinkles and six grandchildren and four step-grandchildren, so I qualify, don't you think? And I sure love you."

That did it. Sarah nodded her head yes, then snuggled in closer. A moment later she asked if I could come by their house and see the goldfish her dad had given her for Christmas. I said I'd be glad to. We went back to their house, looked at the fish and played a game.

As I was walking out the door after saying good-bye, she called after me with joy in her voice: "Bye, Grandma. I love you!"

While walking home I thought, Lord, what have I done? I'm afraid I acted out of compassion in the moment, but I don't know if I can keep this commitment. We already have so many grand-kids of our own. Then ever so gently I sensed the Holy Spirit impressing on me that God had assigned me this special job and He would give me all the resources I needed to do it.

It has been several years since that incident and I have never once felt a lack of love or grace to keep my commitment. God is faithful. My heart is full of gratitude for my two "adopted" grandchildren.

WORDS TO REFLECT ON

Come, my children, listen to me; I will teach you the fear of the LORD. —PSALM 34:11

Enlarge the place of your tent, stretch your tent curtains wide, do not hold back; lengthen your cords, strengthen your stakes. —ISAIAH 54:2

Therefore, my brothers, be all the more eager to make your calling and election sure. For if you do these things, you will never fall. —2 PETER 1:10

LOOKING WITHIN, LIVING IT OUT

- What opportunity has God presented you with that you have been afraid to accept?
- How has your reluctance to obey kept you from expressing praise and gratitude?

- What can you do even today to reverse this pattern?
- Thank God in writing for an opportunity He has set before you. Accept it by His grace. Then drop your paper into your Blessing Basket.

PRAYER STARTER

Lord, thank you for providing me with opportunities to share with those in need the love you have poured into my life. I want to continue to say "yes" to you and to receive the grace to carry out your call—whatever it might be. I receive so much more than I give. I praise you for continuing to challenge me to enlarge and stretch myself and not to hold back.

Being Grateful for What We Take for Granted

 WE ARISE IN the morning, jump in the shower, pop a slice of bread in the toaster, turn on the coffee-maker, pick up the newspaper outside our front door, boot up the computer to look at the stock market action and check our e-mail.

Later we jump into our car and speed off to work. Everything we need is waiting for us: an elevator to take us to the designated floor with just a push of a button, a desk and chair, overhead lights, a fax and phone, a copy machine so we can duplicate whatever work we turn out that day.

On the way home we stop at the gym, lift weights, ride the stationary bicycle, sweat in the sauna, cool down in the shower. We drop by the supermarket and pluck our favorite foods off the shelves and out of the freezer.

We dash home, grab a pot and pan or pop a prepared dinner into the microwave, then flip on the TV to watch the news or a sitcom. Or maybe we listen to a classical CD and plop down by the fireplace with a satisfying book. Then we're off to bed. It feels good to settle down on a comfortable mattress with a fluffy quilt to warm us. Just think! An entire day filled with comforts and conveniences that most of us take entirely for granted.

But sometimes the very items that make our lives easier can also be our undoing. Instead of inspiring gratitude within us, they stir up irritation. They require assembly and maintenance, training and practice, and eventually repair and replacement. We aren't satisfied. We want more—we want perfection—and we won't say thanks until we have it.

On the other hand, some of us become so dependent on these gifts of technology that we lose sight of the Giver. And still others dismiss their value, preferring instead to live "above" the things of the world.

But if God is first in our lives—He is first—period. Our priorities will be in order. We will receive His gifts of technology and use them appropriately. Whether at a keyboard or an ironing board, lifting weights or tilling the soil, we can remain aware of the One who made them all possible. Then our natural response will be one of praise and thanks for every good thing.

WORDS TO REFLECT ON

He grants peace to your borders and satisfies you with the finest of wheat. —PSALM 147:14

You will have plenty to eat, until you are full, and you will praise the name of the LORD your God, who has worked wonders for you; never again will my people be shamed. —JOEL 2:26

I will heal their waywardness and love them freely, for my anger has turned away from them. —HOSEA 14:4

LOOKING WITHIN, LIVING IT OUT

- What gifts have you taken for granted?
- What specifically do you want to thank God for today that you have previously overlooked?
- How can paying closer attention to the little things help you cultivate a more grateful heart?
- List the things you've been inclined to take for granted. Thank God for them. Then drop your paper into your Blessing Basket.

127

PRAYER STARTER

Lord God, there are so many things to be grateful for each day, things I often take for granted—like hot water for my shower, electricity to heat and light my home, a hot bagel and coffee to take off the morning chill, a comfortable bed to sleep in, a phone and fax machine and computer to transport my personal and business affairs— so many things I use and enjoy but forget to give thanks for. I want to change that today, Lord. I want to be open to every gift, however large or small. They all come from your hand. I praise and thank you for your provision in every area of my life.

Rejoicing in Relationships

ONE CANNOT measure or weigh the gift of relationship. It is one of the great intangibles of life. Whether you give or receive, there is no mistaking its power to touch and bless and heal. The gift of yourself is the greatest gift you can give. The gift of another to you is the greatest gift you can receive. To experience an intimate relationship is to experience profound gratitude, for there is no substitute—except God Himself—for the love and care of another person.

I learned this early in life from my mother and father. Our home was full of people: aunts, uncles and cousins, friends old and new, neighbors and coworkers, nuns and priests, grandparents and grandchildren. And when guests couldn't come to us, my parents went to them.

I'll never forget my emotion on my fortieth birthday as I entered the restaurant where my husband had planned a party for me. The room was filled with loving friends, flowers and music, and a large display of photographs, spanning my life. I hurried from one table to the next, greeting each guest. Then suddenly at the back of the room I spotted a gentle, smiling man with a vibrant, blue-eyed woman on his arm.

"Mom! Dad!" I gasped. They had flown to California from Illinois just hours before. I burst into tears at the sight of these two who, more than anyone else, had taught me the value of relationship and the importance of gratitude.

In that moment I gave thanks—not just for the party and flowers and music and food, wonderful as all of it was. What really touched me was the sight of men and women, young and old, smiling at me from all parts of the room: my family, friends, neighbors, tennis partners, writing colleagues. What a sight! A room filled with dear ones who had come to celebrate me, to acknowledge me, to say thanks for me. It took my breath away.

Some years later my husband and I received an invitation to an unusual wedding. Our friends had been married years before in a civil ceremony, and they wanted to re-affirm their commitment to one another in a sacred service. We were preparing to leave on a trip the following day so I considered not going to the wedding. There was so much to do! I called Margaret to explain my dilemma, to beg off. But at the sound of my voice, she said, "Karen, you're coming, aren't you?"

I hesitated but then recalled the sight of my parents at my birthday party. And I thought about my friends: Ann who saw me through an illness, my sister who was there for me during my divorce, my friend Geri who stuck by me while I learned to play tennis—people who demonstrated their love by staying in relationship with me.

"Yes, Margaret, of course we'll be there," I said. We went. And I'm so grateful we did. Margaret's in-laws didn't make it. Her two grown sons were absent, and her sister, ill with cancer, couldn't be there. My husband and I were among her dearest guests.

Sometimes giving and receiving closeness not only blesses us—it also challenges us. I remember an elderly neighbor who nursed her terminally ill husband for two years. I dropped off a card from time to time, an encouraging note, a single rose in a little vase. But I'm ashamed to say, I didn't go in and talk or pray with her.

Then one morning a note appeared under our door. "Karl went to heaven last night at 10:30." I didn't know what to do so I did what was comfortable: I left a sympathy card by her door. A few days later we met, unexpectedly, in the lobby of our building. There she stood: frail, exhausted, lonely.

"Phyllis," I whispered, surprised at the impact of our meeting. As our eyes met, we reached for one another like two children. We went up to her apartment and talked for over an hour. I had not been there for her during Karl's last days, but she needed me now, and finally I was there.

WORDS TO REFLECT ON

I am a friend to all who fear you, to all who follow your precepts. —PSALM 119:63

Now about brotherly love we do not need to write to you, for you yourselves have been taught by God to love each other. —1 THESSALONIANS 4:9

But Martha was distracted by all the preparations that had to be made. She came to him and asked, "Lord, don't you care that my sister has left me to do the work by myself? Tell her to help me!" "Martha, Martha," the Lord answered, "you are worried and upset about many things, but only one thing is needed. Mary has chosen what is better, and it will not be taken away from her."
—LUKE 10:40–42

LOOKING WITHIN, LIVING IT OUT

- How have your relationships increased your gratitude?
- What are some of the significant blessings that have come to you through your loved ones?
- How can you express your gratitude for them in tangible ways?
- Write a prayer of gratitude for the most significant relationships in your life and add it to your Blessing Basket.

131

PRAYER STARTER

Lord Jesus, thank you for the gift of relationships, including relatives, friends, coworkers, roommates, neighbors—people who stand with me, pray for me, laugh and cry with me, pay attention to me. I am so grateful for these dear people who contribute to my life day in and day out. I know they are a reflection of the great love you have for me. How I thank you for that gift!

Thanking God for Darkness and Light

 MATT WAS between jobs, between relationships, basically "between a rock and a hard place" as he put it. "I needed to get away, to think and pray and get some direction for my life." He heard about a men's retreat at a lake not far from where he lived, and it sounded like the perfect solution to his dilemma.

Matt arrived on a Friday afternoon, selected a bunk, unloaded his duffel and headed for the lake. "I spotted a trail and decided to see where it led. I walked around the entire lake watching the birds, swimmers and boaters. It was so peaceful I didn't want to come back."

Matt says he took a break on a high rock and sat down to pray. "I asked the Lord to make this weekend count for something more than just a few hours away from home. I wanted to leave with a plan for my life."

By Saturday afternoon Matt became anxious. He wondered if God had heard him, much less cared. That night he dropped into a prayer-and-fellowship meeting after dinner. "I stayed for about an hour and then excused myself and started down the path to my cabin. It was pitch black. Not even a sliver of moon showed through the trees. I suddenly felt scared. It was the oddest feeling. There I was, an adult male, used to being on my own and not easily intimidated, but that night I was afraid to walk alone. My cabin was situated in the trees some distance from the lodge, and frankly, I wasn't sure which way to go."

Matt says he felt like a child, sorry he hadn't waited for a buddy to walk with him. "I started to pray. I told the Lord I was scared and felt lost. I started shivering even though it was a warm evening." Matt flicked on his penlight, but it made little more than a dime-sized spot at his feet. I need more light than this, he thought, feeling frustrated.

133

"No sooner had I closed my mouth than I had the answer to my prayer. It was so obvious I laughed out loud. I had enough light—enough for a footstep at a time. How much more did I need? I thought of what God had told Isaiah about the people of Israel. He'd lead them in paths they hadn't known before, and He'd make darkness light before them. I got back to my cabin and crashed.

"I woke up Sunday morning and knew with certainty that the direction I sought, like the light, would come when I needed it— one step at a time. I drove home that day thanking God for the light—and for the darkness, too."

WORDS TO REFLECT ON

You, O LORD, keep my lamp burning; my God turns my darkness into light. —PSALM 18:28

He reveals the deep things of darkness and brings deep shadows into the light. —JOB 12:22

Therefore, if your whole body is full of light, and no part of it dark, it will be completely lighted, as when the light of a lamp shines on you. —LUKE 11:36

134

LOOKING WITHIN, LIVING IT OUT

- What part of your heart or path is still in darkness?
- Have you rejected or accepted the light God has shown you? In what way?
- Have you allowed dark thoughts to replace words of gratitude?
- Write down some of the ways God has shed light on the dark areas of your life. Thank Him for them and add your paper to your Blessing Basket.

PRAYER STARTER

Dear God, thank you for the darkness, for without it, I wouldn't see the importance of the light—and I would likely become so self-sufficient that I wouldn't turn to you for direction, for comfort, for help. Thank you, too, for the light—Jesus Christ—the Light of the world, who makes darkness light for me.

Giving Thanks Year Round

AS WE DEVELOP a more grateful heart, we'll soon see every day as Thanksgiving Day. Not a moment will pass that we don't notice something to be grateful for. Giving thanks will come naturally. We'll not only give thanks for the perfect parking place, but also for the friendly checker at the grocery store, for that last postage stamp in the drawer just when we need it, for enough mustard to spread on the turkey in our sandwich, for the cute little dog next door we can play with but don't have to clean up after! Gratitude will become a way of life.

It will deepen and settle into us like a hot cup of soup, filling us with warmth and strength that will see us through the tough times. That is when our attitude of gratitude can really serve us. We will be able to see the blessings behind the pain of death or divorce, the hurt of judgment and disappointment or the loss of a relationship we counted on.

Jesus Christ will be in these places with us, filling us with grace and peace and serenity because we will know from past experience that everything works together for good to those who love Him. With this reality to shore us up, we cannot help but feel grateful for whatever comes our way.

One late October morning, Charles and I discovered this as we began planning our family Thanksgiving. "This year, let's do something different," I said.

"How about having dinner at the cottage?" Charles suggested. "Of course, it'll mean more work." It was true we didn't have all the conveniences at our cabin that we had in our city apartment—like a dishwasher and a reliable oven and a big table. But so what, I mused, neither did the Pilgrims.

"Let's do it," I said. On Thanksgiving morning my husband and I arrived before the rest of the family and set out a few surprises. We had filled colorful lunch bags with a variety of treats—chewing gum, nuts, raisins, coins, travel-sized toiletries, small toys for the kids—then tied them with bright string and hung them from the log beams in the living room. We also attached a personal thank-you note to each one, expressing our love and gratitude.

When everyone arrived, we sat in a circle by the fire, sipped sparkling cider, talked and prayed and shared our potluck dinner and the surprise bags. Then each person—even the youngest—took a turn voicing the blessings he or she was grateful for.

"What a great day!" my husband commented as we packed the car the next morning. "I wish this feeling of gratitude and love could last all year."

"But it can," I said. "We made this day special simply by choosing to. What's to stop us from making every day just as special?"

136

We decided to make a point of keeping the spirit of Thanksgiving all year round. We weren't exactly certain how we'd do it, but we were committed. While driving home, we realized it hadn't been the food, the fire, the games or the mountain cabin that had made our Thanksgiving special.

It was the people—each one so dear and unique. We decided then and there to phone more often, stop by and visit, share a favorite recipe or drop a card in the mail. Reaching out to others in these and other small ways has kept us firmly planted on the ground of gratitude all the years since. I do feel now that Thanksgiving is a year-round affair.

WORDS TO REFLECT ON

137

He is like a tree planted by streams of water, which yields its fruit in season and whose leaf does not wither. Whatever he does prospers. —PSALM 1:3

A generous man will himself be blessed, for he shares his food with the poor. —PROVERBS 22:9

Each man should give what he has decided in his heart to give, not reluctantly or under compulsion, for God loves a cheerful giver. And God is able to make all grace abound to you, so that in all things at all times, having all that you need, you will abound in every good work. As it is written: "He has scattered abroad his gifts to the poor; his righteousness endures forever." —2 CORINTHIANS 9:7–9

LOOKING WITHIN, LIVING IT OUT

- What action could you take today to demonstrate your appreciation and thanks to someone close to you?
- How would your life be different if you made every day a celebration of thanks?
- What are some of the ways people bless you with gifts of love and kindness?
- Write down two things you are especially grateful for today and put them into your Blessing Basket.

PRAYER STARTER

God, I thank you today for your continuous provision. You not only take care of my physical needs, but you also feed my spirit. You give ear to my words. You consider my meditation. You heed my cry. You are my refuge in times of trouble. You show me the path of life. Your presence is full of joy. At your right hand are eternal pleasures. I bow before you in praise and gratitude, my King and my God.

Discovering Hidden Treasure

 HAVE YOU EVER come to a point where you were so fed up you couldn't imagine going on? Maybe you weren't able to put your finger on the frustration. You just knew things were all wrong and you didn't know what to do about them.

Maureen talked with me about such a time in her life. "I remember when my life felt like a giant landfill!" she said. "Everywhere I looked I saw a huge bag of trash. Finances—I wished I had more money. Marriage—I wished my husband did things my way. Family relationships—I wished my parents and kids were more supportive. Friendships—I wished people were more thoughtful."

Wish. Wish. Mumble. Complain. Maureen admitted she couldn't find anything to be happy about. To get away from it all—at least for a day—she ran off to the desert with a group of walkers. A good workout was just what she needed to gain some perspective.

After the first hour on a long trail to a distant grove of palm trees, Maureen said she felt overcome by the heat reflecting off miles of unrelenting sand. "I sat down on a rock, gulped water thirstily and poured the rest of the bottle over my head!" she said, laughing. "I was ready to call it quits and head for my cool car. I hadn't come here to be burned up and burned out, but something urged me to press on."

As the group drew closer to the oasis of thick, healthy palm trees, Maureen's viewpoint began to shift. What a paradise that lay before them. In what seemed like the middle of nowhere, she heard the gurgle of a gentle stream, saw large plots of shade under the waving fronds, and plenty of places to sit and rest from the dizzying heat.

"And to think I had almost given up, turned back and driven off in a huff," she added, "disappointed once more because things weren't going the way I wanted them to."

Maureen admitted she felt ashamed of her selfish thoughts and self-centered point of view. "I knew God was speaking to me," she said, "calling me aside for a heart-to-heart conversation. It was clear I needed a good 'talking to,' as my mother used to say."

She sat down, took off her boots, dipped her feet and neckerchief into the cool water and rested in God's presence. As the water relieved the heat, God's gentle prodding brought relief to Maureen's weary mind.

"I felt Him encouraging me to take a look at these good folks who were here with me, my companions and fellow-walkers who loved the outdoors, appreciated nature and who enjoyed the friendship of others with this common interest. What a privilege it was just to be here. My lungs and legs worked. My feet had carried me without complaining. My heart accepted the extra burden. How blessed I was simply to be," she said.

Then Maureen thought about her family, her husband who supported her unselfishly with his time and energy—even if his ways were not always her ways, her children and grandchildren who brought such joy into her life, and her work as an artist.

"I was living my dream," she said, "doing what I loved to do and what God had called me to do. Maybe I didn't have all the money I'd like to have, but I had enough. I was never without anything I really needed. I had good health, a comfortable home, a car that worked, and a family and church community that nurtured me."

By the time Maureen finished musing the list of blessings God had poured into her life, she realized she not only had nothing to complain about, she had everything to be thankful for.

"And to think I almost missed these gifts," she said, "all because I was too focused on my own expectations. I came home that day a different person—a grateful person. What I had seen as trash, God had shown me was really hidden treasure."

WORDS TO REFLECT ON

Show the wonder of your great love, you who save by your right hand those who take refuge in you from their foes. —PSALM 17:7

He will be the sure foundation for your times, a rich store of salvation and wisdom and knowledge; the fear of the LORD is the key to this treasure. —ISAIAH 33:6

> For where your treasure is, there your heart will be also.
> —LUKE 12:34

LOOKING WITHIN, LIVING IT OUT

- What does Scripture mean when it says the key to the treasure which is God begins with the fear of the Lord?
- What do you most treasure? Is that treasure reflected in the attitude of your heart?
- What might you do this week to refresh yourself, to be still, and to rest in God's presence?
- Consider the "treasures" in your life (God's love, family, friends, nature and so on). Then write down the names of specific people or experiences and put the slips into your Blessing Basket.

PRAYER STARTER

Dear God, I am so grateful for the gift of your Son, Jesus Christ, the greatest treasure of all. Without His saving grace I would be lost. But today I am joyful and thankful because of what He did for me on the Cross. Thank you for showing me again and again that my life is a treasure chest, not a landfill! You have given me life itself, food for my table, a roof over my head, a family to love and enjoy, provision for all my needs, and friends to share the journey. Help me today to be mindful of all these blessings so that in all my affairs I will, in turn, be a blessing to others. I love You, Lord, and I know you love me.

Bouncing Back From Pain and Problems

ABRAHAM BOUNCED back from disbelief when God brought him a son in the late years of his life. The Samaritan woman at the well bounced back from deceit and adultery when she met Jesus, the Messiah, and received His "living water." And Zacchaeus, the tax collector, bounced back from cheating when he offered to pay back four times the amount of money he took dishonestly.

Over the years, Burt had read and heard these accounts at church and in his own reading of Scripture, but he did not understand the gift of God's grace personally, until he went through a wrenching divorce when his children were young.

Burt says he grew up with criticism and he became a critic himself. "I was so emotionally entangled with my father," he said, "I couldn't think for myself. I continually looked for my dad's approval—even though I never received it."

As an adult he tried to cover his pain with alcohol. "I remember when my kids were young," he said, "I took the family only to places where I knew I could get a drink."

Despite Burt's problem with his own father, he admits with dismay, "I treated my kids the same way. I was critical of everything they did." His greatest regret is not realizing the extent of the damage until they were grown. His daughter struggled for a time with being overweight and his son often escaped into sports and work.

But when he speaks of their relationship today, his words are warm and his eyes brighten. After a recent visit with his daughter, where they really talked for the first time, he received a note from her saying how great it was to get to know him.

"I'm finally learning to do things differently with my children than my father did with me," he said. "When they ask what I think about a particular situation, I give an example from my life and share the result. I don't advise and criticize anymore."

Burt also admits freely that none of this would be possible without God being present in his life. "I'm just as human as anyone," he said, "but as a Christian, I now take responsibility for my actions in a way I never did before I knew the Lord."

As Burt focuses on the present and trusts God for his future, he knows the freedom of bouncing back from regret, from anger and from guilt. Today he gives thanks for all of it.

WORDS TO REFLECT ON

The LORD is my rock, my fortress and my deliverer; my God is my rock, in whom I take refuge. He is my shield and the horn of my salvation, my stronghold. —PSALM 18:2

"Nevertheless, I will bring health and healing to it; I will heal my people and will let them enjoy abundant peace and security." —JEREMIAH 33:6

. . . how God anointed Jesus of Nazareth with the Holy Spirit and power, and how he went around doing good and healing all who were under the power of the devil, because God was with him. —ACTS 10:38

LOOKING WITHIN, LIVING IT OUT

- What pain or problem in your life needs the touch of God? What would you most like Him to do for you in that area so you can bounce back?
- Do you have a critical or supportive spirit? Write down an example of either one.
- What Scripture verse would help you focus on bouncing back from pain rather than dwelling in it?
- List three things you are grateful for that have resulted from the pain in your life. Drop that paper into your Blessing Basket.

PRAYER STARTER

Dear God, I know you are the Great Physician of the body, mind and spirit. Please help me today to focus on bouncing back rather than wallowing in my pain and problems. You promise to bring good out of whatever comes into my life. I want to live in that promise, beginning right now. I pray for your strength and guidance as I take action, looking for the positive side of each experience so I can glorify you and be a witness of your love and grace in the lives of other people.

Starting Over

SOME PEOPLE experience a new beginning at the end of their life. They wait until it has fallen apart completely before they make a fresh start, before they realize with gratitude God's gift to His people in the person of Jesus Christ. That happened to a man I'll call Tim. He married his wife, Phyllis, in the early 1930s, graduated from law school with honors, established a respectable law firm and drew favorable clients. Phyllis worked in his office and helped him build the business.

Soon they began living a fast-paced life, drinking heavily and attending social events several nights a week. They had new cars each year, fancy vacations and expensive clothing. They were pleased with what they had accomplished on their own. Tim, a self-professed atheist, liked to joke about the fact that he didn't need any help from God!

Then suddenly one day some ten years later, everything changed. Phyllis accepted an invitation from a friend to visit a Bible study forming in their neighborhood. After just one meeting, she came home visibly shaken. Something was different about her. She told Tim she had heard the truth that day—Jesus Christ had died for her sins. She had prayed and had asked Him to take over her life and to forgive her sins. Phyllis bubbled with excitement about this deep change within her, and she hoped Tim would join her and start going to church with her.

But Tim didn't want any part of his wife's newfound religion. In fact, he was angry that Phyllis upset their life with her outlandish decision. He resisted everything the Christian faith stood for. He shut out Phyllis from that point on—although they remained married for another 40 years.

Tim's life changed again when he and Phyllis could no longer live alone. Their daughter moved them to a nursing home where Tim lingered for several months after a severe fracture. He lived in one wing and Phyllis roomed alone in another wing. Tim did not speak to her, visit her or accept her attempts to see him.

Hank, a minister and friend of Phyllis', dropped by her room often just to talk, and he stopped to speak with Tim, too. The two men struck up a friendship. When Hank died of cancer later that year Tim was devastated. Marjorie, a friend of Hank's, had come by to share the news.

She told Tim right out, "Hank is with Jesus. He put his life in God's hands many years ago—just as Phyllis did. One thing he wanted more than anything else was for you to know Jesus, too," she said. "Do you know where you're going when your time is up?" she asked gently. "I'd like to talk to you about what God promised through Jesus—if you'll let me."

Tim's eyes were wet with tears as he nodded yes. Marjorie shared the Gospel and Tim gave his life to Christ that day. The following morning Tim died peacefully. His life had fallen apart, but God granted him a new beginning—in heaven. All Tim had to do was say "yes" to Jesus.

WORDS TO REFLECT ON

He rescued me from my powerful enemy, from my foes, who were too strong for me. —PSALM 18:17

Though we are slaves, our God has not deserted us in our bondage. He has shown us kindness in the sight of the kings of Persia: He has granted us new life to rebuild the house of our God and repair its ruins, and he has given us a wall of protection in Judah and Jerusalem. —EZRA 9:9

We were therefore buried with him through baptism into death in order that, just as Christ was raised from the dead through the glory of the Father, we too may live a new life. —ROMANS 6:4

LOOKING WITHIN, LIVING IT OUT

- Have you prayed for someone in your life for a long time, yet not seen any fruit? Who is that person and what do you long for in your relationship with him or her?
- What do you believe God wants you to do about this situation?
- What have you learned about God through this trial of what appears to be unanswered prayer?
- Jot down two things the Lord has shown you about yourself and about the person you're praying for. Give thanks for this revelation and write them down and place them into your Blessing Basket.

PRAYER STARTER

Dear God, sometimes I feel like St. Augustine's mother.
I've been praying for my son and my husband for more
than thirty years, but I don't see any changes in their
hearts. Or is it my heart that hasn't changed? Maybe I'm
the one who's become hardened because I don't see an
answer to my prayer—or at least the kind of answer I
want. Forgive me, Lord, for giving up so easily. What is
twenty or thirty years of prayer compared to eternity?
My task is to pray. The results are yours. May I keep
that in mind as I bring my husband and son before you
again today, asking that they hear your voice and call
on your name.

Befriending the Friendless

 SOMETIMES WHILE we are simply minding our own business, a person comes along and upsets the status quo. We meet the man or woman we will marry. We hold our first baby in our arms. We meet a man or a woman at work or in our neighborhood and find ourselves face to face with an opportunity to express God's love in a way we've never done before.

My husband Charles experienced such a challenge when he met a man named Dan while working his new job as a shoe salesman at a major department store in Southern California. To most people—even members of his own family—Dan was a "standoffish, suspicious, aloof man," said Charles. "He related to people only when they needed something from him."

Charles spoke wistfully of this odd man who worked alongside him for ten years. Dan was the store's "shoeshine man."

"He had learned well how to refinish and refurbish shoes," added Charles. "And he liked it when people needed his services—when he could help in some way."

Charles could tell the day they met that Dan had few friends. He and his grown children were estranged, and Dan's crusty exterior created a barrier between him and other employees. But Charles sensed that beneath the surface lived a man who was frightened and very needy. Charles decided to befriend Dan.

He began kidding with him, talking to him about customers, the weather, politics, whatever came up between them. Charles also gave each of his shoe customers a coupon for a complimentary shine. Soon a steady flow of regular and return customers stopped by Dan's shoeshine stand located at the edge of the shoe department. Not only did Charles reach out to Dan, but also before long Dan began reaching out to customers—offering a bit of extra service and inviting them back!

Charles smiled as he recalled the gradual changes that occurred as a result of this simple act of initiating a friendship.

"We were close to the same age," said Charles, "so right there we had something in common. Dan loved to talk about 'the good old days' and he was happy to have someone in the store he could relate to. He also liked to complain that the world was no longer the same as it once was."

He had a sad, negative bent, but at the same time he could be funny and liked to spar. Charles laughed as he talked about Dan's typical morning greeting. "How're you doing, you ugly puss?! Gosh you're a mean looking dude. Don't know why I put up with you. You're just lucky, I guess!"

Charles laughed it off and shot back with a playful comment of his own. "We carried on this way for days at a time," he said.

"I overlooked a lot in Dan," said Charles. "Perhaps he did the same with me. I found it hard to be around him sometimes. He'd get on a topic that bugged him and suddenly all the hate and disappointment bottled up inside would spill onto whoever was standing there."

Charles chuckled as he described Dan as a "handful." "He'd get tangled up in a subject or problem and then be mad at me." But Charles did not apologize for something he had no part in. "Instead I challenged him by asking hard questions that made him think. 'Do you want to end our friendship this way?' I'd ask. Then he'd back down and make a joke."

Charles admitted it was a chore to contend with Dan, but the man had few people he could even get mad at, so Charles took it in stride—instead of personally. "If I had let him get to me, the friendship would have ended," said Charles, "and neither of us wanted that."

Charles said he felt sad when he realized Dan had been the culprit in his own life. He had cut out the love he could have had because he was too stubborn to forgive, to receive forgiveness and to made amends.

Without realizing it, however, Dan was the catalyst for some deep spiritual growth in Charles. "I have such a rich life," said Charles. "Surely I could share some of it. I'm so grateful for the Lord's love and faithfulness to me. Dan seemed indifferent to religion. Perhaps he was mad at God. He also felt bad about himself, about his life—even though he was too proud to admit it."

On occasion Dan would talk about how much his family had disappointed him, but almost never about the mistakes he had made with them. He was the classic victim. But Charles did not withhold his love. And over time it trickled back.

153

On two occasions, Dan surprised Charles by purchasing tickets for the two of them to attend a piano concert and an evening of comedy with Red Skelton.

Then on Dan's seventieth birthday, something important occurred. Charles ordered a cake from the bakery in the store cafe, and passed word to all the employees to gather in the lunch room to sing "Happy Birthday" to Dan and enjoy a slice of cake. Dan had no idea what the staff was up to. He likely thought his birthday would be just another day like so many others in his lonely life.

He nearly collapsed with surprise when he walked into the lunchroom that day. Balloons, colored plates, a beautiful cake and dozens of smiling employees were in place, waiting for his arrival.

"It was a priceless moment," said Charles. "I believe there was a shift inside Dan that day. From time to time he would talk about what that celebration meant to him, but still it was difficult for him to express his true feelings."

Six months later Charles received a call from Debbie, the human resources manager at the store. Dan had died quietly in his sleep the night before. Debbie knew Charles would want to be among the first to know. Everyone in the store was aware of their unusual but special friendship.

"I learned some important lessons by simply observing Dan's life," said Charles. "I owe him a lot. I loved the guy," he added, choking up a bit at the memory of "Dan, the shoeshine man."

"It was easy to love him. He had so little. It never cost me a thing. He gave me more than he ever knew. I thank God for his life and the imprint it made on mine."

WORDS TO REFLECT ON

Do not let the oppressed retreat in disgrace; may the poor and needy praise your name. —PSALM 74:21

If there is a poor man among your brothers in any of the towns of the land that the LORD your God is giving you, do not be hardhearted or tight-fisted toward your poor brother. —DEUTERONOMY 15:7

"He who despises his neighbor sins, but blessed is he who is kind to the needy." —PROVERBS 14:21

LOOKING WITHIN,
LIVING IT OUT

- Are there some unusual people in your life? If so, who are they and what makes them different?
- What might you do to bring them God's love and acceptance?
- How has one or more of these people been a blessing in disguise to you? Be as specific as possible.
- Jot down one or two things about each person for which you are grateful and put the paper into your Blessing Basket.

PRAYER STARTER

Dear God, maybe I'm an unusual person in the life of someone else, and I don't even know it. I look at others through my own lens of what is acceptable and right and appropriate. I forget I have only one point of view and others may not share it. Imagine that! It makes me smile to think of how arrogant I've been, judging others when I should be judging myself. Please help me reach out to someone in need of a friend and to be the person you'd have me be—at least for today.

Loving Over the Long Haul

LAST SUMMER my husband and I received an invitation to a dinner party at the home of our friends, Corinne and Ed. It would not be an ordinary party, however. It was to be a celebration of the couple's fiftieth wedding anniversary. We could hardly wait to attend. It was a milestone in the lives of these dear people, and we wanted to be there to honor and give thanks for them.

As guests arrived we went to the garden where beautifully decorated tables with fresh flowers, colorful tableware and pretty party napkins awaited us. Festive punch, hot appetizers and warm conversation added to the pre-dinner hour. Before and after the meal we sauntered through their home, taking time to look at photos of Corinne and Ed and their children at various stages in their family life. Their wedding album lay open on the coffee table in the living room. Everyone crowded around, curious to see what they looked like and what they wore on that special day half a century ago.

The tribute to two people who have modeled commitment in their lives and in the lives of all who know them deeply moved me. I wished young married couples, those engaged and people who are dating with an eye to getting married, could have been there to see the visible signs of what it means to love over the long haul—regardless of the challenges.

Some time later I asked Corinne what has kept them together. She told me keeping the Lord first in her life has helped her sustain her commitment to her husband through the tough times. "Whenever we face difficulties we stop and remember how God has taken care of us in the past," she said. "He's been with us through difficulties again and again. He has proven himself worthy."

Fifty years with one person is a long time! Yet the years can become sweeter as they add up because of the intimacy that comes through shared history, creating a family together, nursing one another through hurts and illness, laughing together (Corinne rated a sense of humor high on her list), and making decisions and choices with the other one in mind.

Ed counts himself a "blessed man." To him, Corinne "is the best wife." He upholds and cherishes her. For some people, such words sound old-fashioned, but every woman should be so graced! Ed's devotion to and gratitude for Corinne was never more evident than at their anniversary party when he wrapped her in loving words and looks during his toast to his bride.

WORDS TO REFLECT ON

The fear of the LORD is pure, enduring forever. The ordinances of the LORD are sure and altogether righteous.
—PSALM 19:9

For this reason a man will leave his father and mother and be united to his wife, and they will become one flesh.
—GENESIS 2:24

But since there is so much immorality, each man should have his own wife, and each woman her own husband.
—1 CORINTHIANS 7:2

LOOKING WITHIN, LIVING IT OUT

- What does "loving over the long haul" mean to you—whether or not you are married?
- How has God demonstrated this phrase in your life?
- What steps can you take today to ensure you will be there for your loved ones—especially your spouse, if you are married—over the long haul?
- List five things you are grateful for about your mate, child, parent or friend and put them into your Blessing Basket.

PRAYER STARTER

Dear God, I don't think I could commit to anyone over the long haul if it weren't for your example of loving me for all eternity. It sounds do-able on one's wedding day or on the day of the birth of a child, but living it out over decades is something else. Everyday there are multiple irritants, issues to face and talk over, clashes of personality and temperament, differences in goals and objectives for our lives together. But there are times of fun and rest and relaxation, too. I don't want to lose sight of those. They, too, are important to loving over the long haul. Today I recommit myself to you, O Lord, and to the people you have given me to love now and in the years to come.

Restoring Broken Relationships with Our Children

 HAVE YOU EVER felt such love for your sons and daughters that you actually went too far in your attempt to advise and protect them? I have. I realized it long afterward how I was interfering in God's work in their lives. Sometimes they have to fall down so He can pick them up and bring them into the only relationship that can make the ultimate difference in their lives—the one with Him.

I discovered through a conversation with a friend, however, that I could become grateful even for my failures.

"I really blew it this time," said Marsha, looking pale and scared as we sat across from each other at our favorite cafe. "I did everything wrong," she continued, "from the minute I walked into Greg's room until I walked out." She folded and unfolded her napkin as she talked.

"He's seventeen years old and has practically nothing to show for it. He doesn't want to go to college. He doesn't really want to work. He's had three part-time jobs in the last year . . . I don't know what to do. Parenting is the hardest thing I've ever done."

"How did he react?" I asked.

"He screamed back as if he hated everything I stood for. He told me to stop running his life. It was frightening. I can still feel his contempt."

Then Marsha reflected on Greg as a little boy.

"Sweet and compliant," she said. "He was a real nice child. I thought we were close. I cooked special meals for him. I picked out this great wallpaper for his room, and I signed him up for soccer and . . ."

My stomach knotted. Marsha sounded like me. Controlling. I remembered imposing my taste and my viewpoint on my children without asking for their input.

"Do you believe in second chances?" Marsha's question startled me back to the present.

"If I didn't, I couldn't go on," I said. "I remember hearing a sermon once about how God is always willing to give us a second chance. If we want to rebuild our relationships with our children of any age, He'll make it possible. It's happening in my life and I know it can happen for you, too."

"But I feel I'm to blame," she said, "even though at the time I thought I was doing the right thing. I took him to church and I helped with his homework and I did things with him—like going to camp and playing baseball."

"But Marsha, wait a minute," I said, suddenly realizing that if parents take all the blame for what didn't work, then shouldn't we take all the credit for what does? And if we do that, aren't we robbing our children of their individuality? They have interests and talents and habits that are entirely their own. Some we like and some we don't.

I shared my discovery with Marsha and she nodded in thought. Then she reached for her purse and gave me a hug. "I've got to run," she said. "You've given me a lot to think about. Thanks so much for listening."

"Thank you," I replied. "You've given me a lot to think about, too."

As I drove home that morning, I was overcome with the idea of second chance parenting—and what that could mean to mothers and fathers who long for the opportunity to restore a troubled or broken relationship with a son or daughter.

And I realized the reality of God's love for me. He had given me a second chance through Jesus Christ. Surely, I thought, such a loving Father wants to redeem my parenting, too.

163

Talking about a second chance, however, can be quite different from living it. It doesn't take much to push our "guilt" button. I can think of numerous ways I've failed—from playing with my children to praying with them, from honesty to intimacy. None of us has been the perfect parent. But the moment such thoughts cross our minds, we have a choice—allowing the guilt and remorse we feel to consume us or turning to God for guidance and forgiveness as we make a new commitment to restore what has been broken.

If you have regrets and remorse over some of your parenting, take heart. It's not too late to begin again. Restoration is not for the arrogant or the prideful. It's for people who are willing to admit their faults and to bring them to the Lord for His grace and guidance. It's for parents who want no less than all God has for them and for their children. Today we have a second chance to look at our relationships in a new way—through the lens of gratitude—so we might praise God for the gift of our sons and daughters and for the grace to renew those relationships with unconditional love.

WORDS TO REFLECT ON

As far as the east is from the west, so far hath he removed our transgressions from us. —PSALM 103:12

When Jesus saw their faith, he said, "Friend, your sins are forgiven." —LUKE 5:20

And the God of all grace, who called you to his eternal glory in Christ, after you have suffered a little while, will himself restore you and make you strong, firm, and steadfast. —1 PETER 5:10

LOOKING WITHIN,
LIVING IT OUT

- Do you have an unresolved issue with one of your children? If so, jot it down and journal about how it started and what it has cost you in terms of intimacy with your son or daughter.
- How has this broken human relationship affected your relationship with God?
- What initial step can you take to begin the healing process?
- List the things which you love and are grateful for about this child and then put that slip into your Blessing Basket.

PRAYER STARTER

Dear God, it breaks my heart when my child and I are at odds with one another. I can only imagine, from this experience, how you feel when your children are separate from you. Now I have a tiny glimpse into the depth of your love for us . . . and for me. You sent your Son, Jesus, to die on the cross in order to bridge that gap so I could have eternal fellowship with you, my heavenly Father. Please help me today to do whatever is necessary and right in restoring my relationship with my estranged child. By your grace, I will do whatever you lead me to do.

Storing Up
Heavenly Treasures

"I NEED A vacation," I told my husband over breakfast one morning.

He looked up from his bowl of cereal and smiled. "Funny you should mention that," he said. "I've been thinking the same thing, but you know we'd have to do it on a budget," he said, looking a bit apologetic.

"That's all right. I just want to get away. How about driving to Death Valley? We could reserve a space at the campground, sleep in our tent and cook over a fire? Doesn't that sound like fun?"

"Sounds great," he said. "Will you look into it for us?"

I got on the phone that morning and made all the arrangements. Within weeks we were on the road heading north from our home in Southern California to Death Valley in Northern California.

Later that day we pulled into the campground, set up our tent and stopped by the Visitors' Center to inquire about what was there to see. "A lot!" said the ranger, with a wide smile. "Depends on how adventurous you are."

"We want to hike and walk and check out the historical sights and . . ."

Before I could finish, she handed us a map, a guide booklet and the local newspaper. Over the next three days I was struck by the incredible hand of God all around us—from sand dunes on the floor of the Valley to snow-capped peaks forming tall boundaries around us, from wildflowers poking up from the dry soil to majestic tree trunks swirled by time and wind, and mile after mile after mile of incredible hills and mountains of every color and formation imaginable.

We also saw the work of man: an abandoned mining sight with the rusty remains of an old water tank in a heap at the bottom of a hill, a pile of rotting boards where a wooden shelter once stood, a deserted road now overgrown with weeds. We visited a ghost town on the Nevada border—a place that once bustled with life but now was lifeless. The evidence of a former time was fast disappearing. Only a few brick and mortar walls remained and part of an old cafe and general store stood against the mountains in the background.

"What a contrast," I said aloud, "what God makes, stands year after year after year and becomes even more beautiful. Look at the mountains and the sand and the flowers and the trees. I can't get enough of them. And look at what happens to man's creation," I added, pointing to the broken windows, the crumbling buildings, the chipped signs, the weed-strewn roads. "Rust and wreckage."

Then suddenly I was aware of God's Word on that very topic. "Do not lay up for yourselves treasures on earth, where moth and rust destroy, and where thieves break in and steal. But lay up for yourselves treasures in heaven, where neither moth nor rust destroy, and where thieves do not break in or steal, for where your treasure is, there will your heart be also" (Matthew 6:19–21).

My husband took my hand. "This is a sad place," he said. "This is what happens when people lay up their treasures on earth. The rush for gold broke many people. We can learn from what we see here."

We drove back to the campground in silence. That night we crawled into our tent, warmed by a simple meal and hot tea, tired but content. As we gazed at the sea of stars overhead and listened to the wind whipping the branches of the tree beside us we were aware of God's presence in a totally new way. We had come to this place on a budget—but we would be going home the next day rich in the treasures of the Lord—"where moth and rust do not destroy . . ." God had blessed us abundantly and we gave thanks.

168

WORDS TO REFLECT ON

How lovely is your dwelling place, O LORD Almighty!
—PSALM 84:1

The kingdom of heaven is like treasure hidden in a field. When a man found it, he hid it again, and then in his joy went and sold all he had and bought that field.
—MATTHEW 13:44

If you then, though you are evil, know how to give good gifts to your children, how much more will your Father in heaven give the Holy Spirit to those who ask him! —LUKE 11:13

LOOKING WITHIN, LIVING IT OUT

- Media advertising focuses on accumulating "treasures" on earth. Which ones have you acquired that have rusted or been ruined by moths?
- What heavenly treasures have you accumulated? How do they differ in value from earthly treasures?
- What heavenly treasures would you like to have more of and why?
- Write a list of the treasures you are grateful for and drop it into your Blessing Basket.

PRAYER STARTER

169

Dear Lord, I thank you for my home and car and job and clothing, and for my "toys" such as my television, cell phone, computer, fax machine, and other worldly possessions. They help me enjoy close communication with other people, and they provide entertainment and relaxation, too. But I know, dear God, that they are only temporal gifts. The ones that really count are oftentimes intangible. I can feel them, but I can't hold them in my hand. Love, for example, is one that comes to mind. Joy is another. And peace, especially the peace that passes all understanding. There is no substitute for such gifts. Thank you for teaching and showing me what really matters and for giving me, most of all, the joy of salvation through Jesus Christ.

Giving Thanks in All Circumstances

LIFE IS DIFFICULT. It's complicated. It's multi-layered. It's unpredictable. It's easy to build resentments. So why give thanks in all circumstances?

I pondered this question as I spoke with various people who, clearly, have done just that. Why have they chosen an affirmative outlook—despite health challenges, disappointments, difficult relationships and the death of loved ones? Because life is easier, more satisfying and, ultimately, more joyful when we embrace it instead of resisting it. Some people call such behavior, "Going with the flow instead of against it." Others see it as surrendering to God—who promises never to leave us or forsake us.

Heather experienced an opportunity to do just that on her twenty-first birthday. She stared at the large box with silver ribbon and the smaller one wrapped in yellow tissue stacked at the edge of the dining room table in her family's home. A bouquet of red and white tea roses lay beside them. Heather picked up the gift card tucked between the stems.

"Happy 21st, honey," it read. "I'm sorry to miss your special day. We'll celebrate together when I get home. Won't be long now. Love, Mom."

Heather said she felt her eyes blur with tears. She had heard those words too often. The day of the mother-daughter banquet at church when she was seven years old. The evening of the parent-student open house in junior high. The day earlier in the year when Heather had made her mother a cake and decorated the house as a surprise for her forty-fifth birthday. But her mother had missed her plane from New Orleans and hadn't made it home till after midnight.

Then as Heather's younger sister, Meg, begged her to open her gifts, Heather forced a smile as she swiped at a tear rolling down her cheek. She looked at the beautiful cake with pink frosting sitting on the glass plate as her father carried it in from the kitchen and placed it on the center of the table. It looked like the one she'd seen at Dessert Cart. Fancy white letters spelled out "HAPPY BIRTHDAY, Heather" and beneath it, "1 Thessalonians 5:18" in small letters.

Heather said it had been her family's custom to put a Scripture verse on each birthday cake. After everyone sang "Happy Birthday," one of her parents would read the passage out loud. This year her father read, "Give thanks in all circumstances, for this is God's will for you in Christ Jesus."

"My dad told me my mother had picked out this verse," said Heather. "It was one of my grandmother's favorites."

Then they talked about her mother's job as a news correspondent and how they had agreed as a family to support her. Still Heather was fighting disappointment, even anger. But then

Heather said she began thinking of how much she and her mother loved one another and how many special times they had shared. Her mother had been at her side the night Heather went to the hospital with pneumonia.

"Nothing could keep me away," her mother had whispered over and over.

Heather also thought about the afternoon she, her mother and grandmother had gone to High Tea at the Garnet Hotel. Her mother had let her wear the pearl heirloom necklace that day—the one Heather had inherited when she turned twelve.

"Suddenly I felt a calm come over me," said Heather. "I remembered the words my dad had read about giving thanks in all circumstances. I decided I could do that. And when my mother returned we could celebrate my birthday all over again."

WORDS TO REFLECT ON

Enter his gates with thanksgiving and his courts with praise. —PSALM 100:4

"Give thanks to the LORD Almighty, for the LORD is good; his love endures forever." —JEREMIAH 33:11

Who is wise and understanding among you? Let him show it by his good life, by deeds done in the humility that comes from wisdom. —JAMES 3:13

LOOKING WITHIN, LIVING IT OUT

- Has someone close to you disappointed you? Not been there when you really needed him or her? Who is that person and what happened to disappoint you?
- What did God show you about this situation?
- What can you do to reverse the downward spiral of thoughts and feelings?
- What are you grateful for even though things have not gone the way you hoped or expected? Write them down and drop them into your Blessing Basket.

PRAYER STARTER

Lord God, it is so difficult to deal with disappointment. Maybe that's because I put so much energy into expectation. I envision the way I want things to turn out—whether a vacation, a relationship, a job or the weather! I want life to "fit my pictures." Sometimes it does and for that I'm thankful. But more often it does not because you have a plan for my ultimate benefit I don't yet see. In order for your will to be done on earth as it is in heaven, certain things must happen in my life. I want to "get" that, O Lord, and to hang on to it. You are God. I'm not. And you are sovereign. I feel better whenever I voice that truth. Thank you for being my Lord and Savior.

Saying Good-bye with a Grateful Heart

GOOD-BYES ARE difficult. When we love people and they obviously love us, none of us wants to say farewell. Most of the time, however, we look forward to another time together so it doesn't seem final. But there are those times when we sense it is a last good-bye.

Such experiences can be sweet and soft if we say good-bye with gratitude. I like to make sure I tell my loved ones how grateful I am for their presence in my life. I want them to remember me as someone who said thank you often, as my mother taught me to do.

This came home to me with renewed depth when I said good-bye to my Kurdish friends who were moving from San Diego to Nashville.

"I love you," Amina whispered between sobs as she kissed me on one cheek, then the other, and hugged me tighter than she ever had in the years we had known one another.

"Bye, Karen," called little Susan, black eyes staring at me out of a round brown face.

"I wish we didn't have to move," shouted 12-year-old Warvin, with his brother Zendon close beside him.

Then I hugged baby Sulein and Amina's husband, Taha.

After this tearful farewell I ran down the steps of their apartment house and hurried to my car. I didn't like this parting moment anymore than they did, but somewhere in my heart I knew God was going ahead of them to Nashville, Tennessee, where they anticipated a better living—a job for Taha, the support of a strong Kurdish community, and a reunion with their two older sons who had gone ahead to find work.

Just three years before, I didn't even know they existed, nor did they know of me. We came together unexpectedly in 1994, the result of an assignment I received from a children's publishing company to write a book for a new series on refugee families who had come to the United States. My task was to locate a Kurdish family, which I did with the help of a religious charity organization in San Diego, California.

Amina Ahmet, Taha Mohammed and their children Khamger, Ferhat, Warvin, and Zendon had settled in the community of El Cajon, east of San Diego, with the help and sponsorship of Amina's half-brother and his wife, following the persecution and encampment of Kurds during the Gulf War. Since their arrival two girls were born into their family, Susan and Sulein.

My relationship with them flourished and continued beyond the completion of the book in 1995. For two years we grew to love one another as family, sharing laughter, conversation, birthday parties, picnics, ethnic foods—even Kurdish dancing!

And then came the unexpected. Taha decided to relocate his family. I was heavy with the thought of losing them, but God is faithful and I have learned to watch for His blessing when I least expect it! And sure enough it came–from another corner of my life where I am an instructor for a correspondence course in writing. During the very time the family was planning their move, a woman named Susan (the same first name as the Amat's youngest daughter) became one of my new students.

In her introductory letter I discovered she lived in Nashville, Tennessee, and her primary interest was working with Kurds! I wrote back immediately and told her about "my family" and specifically about the older boys, Khamger and Ferhat, who had moved to Nashville only months before. She responded right away. She knew them. They had become her friends!

Oh Lord, can this be you? I prayed. What a blessing! Later when I told Susan the rest of the family would be moving to Nashville and needed help enrolling the children in school and becoming familiar with housing, grocery stores, freeways, etc., she offered to step in, gladly, she said, assuring me she would pick up with this family where I and others had left off.

A few weeks after the family moved, Susan reported Taha had a job washing dishes in a restaurant. It wasn't much, but it was a start. The younger children were enrolled in school and teachers were impressed with their English and academic skills, and Amina was finding her way around town with Susan's help.

When I think of this precious family I am at once sad—for I miss them terribly—and thankful, because I know God has His hand on their lives. Though they once walked in the midst of trouble—out of Kurdistan and into the United States—it was not without purpose. God stretched out His hand against their foes and delivered them. And I am most grateful to them for their gift of love in my life and to God for bringing us together.

WORDS TO REFLECT ON

Then they cried to the LORD in their trouble, and he saved them from their distress. —PSALM 107:19

In all their distress he too was distressed, and the angel of his presence saved them. In his love and mercy he redeemed them; he lifted them up and carried them all the days of old. —ISAIAH 63:9

But we ought always to thank God for you, brothers loved by the Lord, because from the beginning God chose you to be saved through the sanctifying work of the Spirit and through belief in the truth. —2 THESSALONIANS 2:13

177

LOOKING WITHIN, LIVING IT OUT

- Is there someone dear to you to whom you've had to say good-bye? What emotions did this parting evoke in you?
- What were you especially grateful for about this individual or family?
- In what ways were you a blessing to these people?
- Jot down some of your favorite memories of time spent with your friends or family and add that paper to your Blessing Basket.

PRAYER STARTER

Dear Lord, how gracious you are to me. You have filled my life with good people who love and care for me, and you have given me a heart of love for them. It's difficult to say farewell. I wish I never had to say good-bye, but no relationship is forever—except the one I have with you. Thank you for your promise that you will never leave me or forsake me, and that you are with me now, and you will be with me throughout eternity.

PART
THREE

CONTINUING
THE JOURNEY

Afterword
Passing It On

"YOU HAVE TO celebrate your chosenness constantly," writes the renowned theologian, Henri Nouwen. "This means saying, 'thank you' to God for having chosen you, and 'thank you' to all who remind you of your chosenness. Gratitude is the most fruitful way of deepening your consciousness that you are not an 'accident,' but a divine choice."[1]

I can't think of a better way to move forward in our quest for a more grateful heart than to continue to say thank you both to God and others, and, in so doing, to realize again and again we are God's people, His chosen ones. Everything we need is within and through Him.

STRETCH YOUR TENT PEGS

After completing this book, your next step might be to move outside your comfort zone and enlarge your ability to give thanks by sharing your experience of gratitude with others and encouraging them to do the same.

AT HOME

- Continue with what you started in this book. Don't stop after forty days. Make gratitude such a part of your life that you continue to add to your Blessing Basket all year long.
- Throw a Praise and Thanksgiving Party. Invite guests to prepare a short personal story about what they are most grateful for.
- Make and decorate Blessing Baskets as gifts for friends and relatives. Share your experience of using your own Blessing Basket.

182

AT CHURCH

- Introduce this activity to members of your church. You might approach your pastor about having Gratitude Sunday or a Thanksgiving Supper where members share publicly the things they are grateful for.
- Create a large, all-church Blessing Basket where members can deposit their gratitude slips. On a selected day various men, women and children could read some of the papers aloud to the congregation and then praise and thank God out loud as a group.
- Plan a day of gratitude for Sunday school where children bring to the classroom someone or something they are grateful for and tell why.

- Offer to help students make individual Blessing Baskets and then introduce them to the process of giving thanks in writing. They can use the baskets in the classroom or take them home to use with their families.

IN YOUR COMMUNITY

- Many schoolteachers have a Thanksgiving feast to celebrate the national holiday in class, but it often centers on food and the history of the first Thanksgiving. You could help children make it personal by offering to create a classroom or school-wide Blessing Basket. The children could add their slips of paper throughout the month of November and then share their blessings aloud in the classroom.
- Suggest a Gratitude Read-a-thon in your community or local school or at a women's or men's group where you belong. Members would bring something to read having to do with giving thanks and share one or more of their own "blessing" experiences. However you choose to expand what you have begun is up to you. The important thing is to do something. In so doing, your sacrifice of thanksgiving honors God, the author and finisher of all good things.

183

Note

1. "Reflections: Classic and Contemporary Excerpts," *Christianity Today*, November 11, 1996, 81.

Personal Pages
Recording Your Blessings

 I INVITE YOU to make the following blank pages your own, to fill them with your thoughts, your individual prayers, your record of special blessings that have come to mind as you've gone through this book. Here is a place to make a permanent record of the things you are most grateful for, to write about them in detail, to preserve them for later reflection or to share with your loved ones. Nineteenth-century American writer Minna Antrim wrote, "Gratitude is the rosemary of the heart." I hope you'll sprinkle the rosemary of your heart on each of these personal pages.

PERSONAL PAGES

Personal Pages

PERSONAL PAGES

PERSONAL PAGES

PERSONAL PAGES